Thinking Education Through Alain Badiou

Educational Philosophy and Theory Special Issue Book Series

Series Editor: Michael A. Peters

The *Educational Philosophy and Theory* journal publishes articles concerned with all aspects of educational philosophy. Their themed special issues are also available to buy in book format and cover subjects ranging from curriculum theory, educational administration, the politics of education, educational history, educational policy, and higher education.

Titles in the series include:

Thinking Education Through Alain Badiou
Edited by Kent den Heyer

Toleration, Respect and Recognition in Education
Edited by Mitja Sardoč

Gramsci and Educational Thought
Edited by Peter Mayo

Patriotism and Citizenship Education
Edited by Bruce Haynes

Exploring Education Through Phenomenology: Diverse Approaches
Edited by Gloria Dall'Alba

Academic Writing, Philosophy and Genre
Edited by Michael A. Peters

Complexity Theory and the Philosophy of Education
Edited by Mark Mason

Critical Thinking and Learning
Edited by Mark Mason

Philosophy of Early Childhood Education: Transforming Narratives
Edited by Sandy Farquhar and Peter Fitzsimons

The Learning Society from the Perspective of Governmentality
Edited by Jan Masschelein, Maarten Simons, Ulrich Bröckling and Ludwig Pongratz

Citizenship, Inclusion and Democracy: A Symposium on Iris Marion Young
Edited by Mitja Sardoc

Postfoundationalist Themes In The Philosophy of Education: Festschrift for James D. Marshall
Edited by Paul Smeyers (Editor), Michael A. Peters

Music Education for the New Millennium: Theory and Practice Futures for Music Teaching and Learning
Edited by David Lines

Critical Pedagogy and Race
Edited by Zeus Leonardo

Derrida, Deconstruction and Education: Ethics of Pedagogy and Research
Edited by Peter Pericles Trifonas and Michael A. Peters

Thinking Education Through Alain Badiou

Edited by
Kent den Heyer

WILEY-BLACKWELL

A John Wiley & Sons, Ltd., Publication

Registered Office

John Wiley & Sons Ltd, The Atrium, Southern Gate, Chichester, West Sussex, PO19 8SQ, United Kingdom

Editorial Offices

350 Main Street, Malden, MA 02148-5020, USA

9600 Garsington Road, Oxford, OX4 2DQ, UK

The Atrium, Southern Gate, Chichester, West Sussex, PO19 8SQ, UK

For details of our global editorial offices, for customer services, and for information about how to apply for permission to reuse the copyright material in this book please see our website at www.wiley.com/wiley-blackwell.

Library of Congress Cataloging-in-Publication data is available for this book.

9781444337426 (paperback)

A catalogue record for this book is available from the British Library.

Set in 10pt Plantin by Toppan Best-set Premedia Limited
Printed and bound in Malaysia by Vivar Printing Sdn Bhd

01   2010

Contents

Notes on Contributors

Charles Barbour is Lecturer in Philosophy at the University of Western Sydney, Australia, and a member of the Centre for Citizenship and Public and Policy; email: c.barbour@uws.edu.au. Along with a number of book chapters, he has published on social and political theory in journals such as *Theory, Culture and Society*, *Philosophy and Social Criticism*, *Law, Culture and the Humanities*, *Telos*, and *The Journal of Classical Sociology*. Most recently, he co-edited, with George Pavlich, a book entitled *After Sovereignty: On the question of political beginnings* (Routledge-Cavendish).

Kent den Heyer is an Associate Professor of social studies and curriculum studies in the Department of Secondary Education, University of Alberta; email: kdenheye@ ualberta.ca. His recent work exploring the implications of Badiou's work for education includes 'Education as an Affirmative Invention: Alain Badiou and the purpose of teaching and curriculum' in *Educational Theory*, 59.4, pp. 441–463 and 'What if Curriculum (of a Certain Kind) Doesn't Matter?' in *Curriculum Inquiry*, 39.1, pp. 27–40.

jan jagodzinski is a Professor in the Department of Secondary Education, University of Alberta in Edmonton, Alberta, Canada, where he teaches visual art and media education and curricular issues as they relate to postmodern concerns of gender politics, cultural studies, and media (film and television); email: jj3@ualberta.ca. He is a founding member of the Caucus on Social Theory in Art Education (NAEA), past editor of *The Journal of Social Theory in Art Education* (JSTAE), past president of SIG Media, Culture and Curriculum, Editorial Board Member for *Psychoanalysis, Culture & Society* (PCS), on the Editorial Advisory Board of *Studies in Art Education* (SAE), *Journal of Curriculum Theorizing* (JCT), *Journal of Cultural Research in Art Education* (JCRAE), and the *Korean Journal of Art Education*, reviewer for *Visual Culture & Gender*, Associate Editor of *Journal of Lacanian Studies* (JLS); and Co-series editor with Mark Bracher of the book series *Pedagogy, Psychoanalysis, Transformation* (Palgrave Press). He is the author of *The Anamorphic I/i* (Duval House Publishing Inc, 1996); *Postmodern Dilemmas: Outrageous essays in art & art education* (Lawrence Erlbaum, 1997); *Pun(k) Deconstruction: Experifigural writings in art & art education* (Lawrence Erlbaum, 1997); Editor of *Pedagogical Desire: Transference, seduction and the question of ethics* (Bergin & Garvey, 2002); *Youth Fantasies: The perverse landscape of the media* (Palgrave, 2004); *Musical Fantasies: A Lacanian approach* (Palgrave, 2005); *Television and Youth: Televised paranoia* (Palgrave, 2008); and *Art and its Education in an era of Designer Capitalism: The deconstruction of the oral eye* (2010).

James G. Henderson is Professor of Curriculum at Kent State University, where he teaches courses in Curriculum Theory, Research, and Leadership; email: jhenders@

kent.edu. He is the coordinator of the college's C&I Master's Degree and PhD programs and co-editor of the *Journal of Curriculum and Pedagogy*. His scholarly interests
focus on democratic curriculum wisdom and its implications for professional development, reflective practice, and curriculum leadership, and he has authored,
co-authored and co-edited four books on these topics, two of which are currently in
their third editions. Currently, he is working with curriculum leaders in Ohio on the
creation of an online Curriculum Leadership Institute.

Kathleen R. Kesson is Professor of Teaching and Learning at the Brooklyn Campus
of Long Island University, where she teaches courses in the foundations of education
and teacher research and coordinates the Childhood Urban Education program;
email: kathleen.kesson@liu.edu. She is co-author, with Jim Henderson, of *Curriculum
Wisdom: Educational decisions in democratic societies* (Prentice Hall, 2004) and *Understanding Democratic Curriculum Leadership* (Teachers College Press, 1999), and editor,
with Wayne Ross, of *Defending Public Schools: Teaching for a Democratic Society* (Praeger,
2004). She is also the author of numerous book chapters, book reviews, and academic
articles in such journals as *Educational Researcher, Teachers College Record, Encounter:
Education for Meaning and Social Justice*, the *Journal of Critical Education Policy Studies,
English Education, Journal of Curriculum Theorizing, Curriculum Inquiry*, and the *Holistic
Education Review*. Her interests are in the areas of democracy in education, critical
pedagogy, aesthetics and education, and teacher inquiry and reflection.

Thomas E. Peterson is Professor of Italian at the University of Georgia; Peterson@
uga.edu. His primary research interests are in the areas of Italian lyric and epic poetry
(Dante, Petrarch, Tasso, Leopardi, Pascoli, the poets of the 20th century) and the
Italian novel. His research in educational philosophy has its origins in his study of
Vico and Whitehead and the process philosophy tradition; current research seeks to
connect that tradition to the work of (among others) Dewey, Peirce, Cassirer, Gregory
and Mary Catherine Bateson, Francisco Varela and Heinz von Foerster.

Anna Strhan is in the process of completing a PhD at the Institute of Education,
London, on conceptualisations of subjectivity and its relation to teaching in the writings of Emmanuel Levinas and Alain Badiou; email: strhan.a@btinternet.com. She
has worked as a teacher of Religious Studies and Philosophy in a range of secondary
schools, and will shortly begin an ethnographic study exploring the formation of
Evangelical lifeworlds in London.

Peter Taubman is a Professor of education in the School of Education at Brooklyn
College; email: PTaubman@brooklyn.cuny.edu. His articles on curriculum, autobio-
graphy, teacher identity, classroom teaching, psychoanalysis and the problems with
standards and accountability have appeared in a range of scholarly journals. He is the
co-author of *Understanding Curriculum* (Peter Lang, 1995) and the author of *Teaching
by Numbers: Deconstructing the discourse of standards and accountability* (Routledge,
2009). He is currently writing a book on psychoanalysis and teaching.

Foreword

ALAIN BADIOU (1937–)[1]

This special issue on the thought of Alain Badiou edited by Kent den Heyer presents the relevance and significance of one of France's most distinguished living philosophers: a student of Althusser, formerly chair of philosophy at the École Normale Supérieure, author of more than twenty books, and a thinker in the Marxist tradition. As an Athusserian Marxist strongly influenced by Lacan, Badiou engaged in fierce debates with both Deleuze and Lyotard in the 1970s. Badiou's (2005) *Being and Event* translated into English seventeen years after its original French publication indicates something of the cultural delay in the reception of his work in the English-speaking world. A work of monumental significance, it has been compared to Heidegger's *Being and Time* and Deleuze's *Difference and Repetition* in its metaphysical outlook and also its willingness to engage with fundamental ontology on the basis of modern set theory with the famous formulation 'mathematics = ontology' (p. 4), which is not a thesis that suggests being is mathematical but rather declares what is expressible of being, and thus is a thesis about discourse.[2] This is also, after structuralism and poststructuralism, some would say a reengagement with the philosophy of the subject and in this sense already a thesis important for politics, art and education, as a number of the contributors to this collection indicate.

As the biography posted on the Faculty Page at the European Graduate School where Badiou teaches notes:

> Trained as a mathematician, Alain Badiou is one of the most original French philosophers today. Influenced by Plato, Georg Wilhelm Friedrich Hegel, Jacques Lacan and Gilles Deleuze, he is an outspoken critic of both the analytic as well as the postmodern schools of thoughts. His philosophy seeks to expose and make sense of the potential of radical innovation (revolution, invention, transfiguration) in every situation.

Unlike many of those schooled in the anti-humanist principles of Louis Pierre Althusser and Jacques Lacan, Alain Badiou has never been tempted to celebrate the apparent end of philosophy, to question the possibility of metaphysics, or to qualify the classical attributes of truth: rigor, clarity, and eternity.

Badiou is someone who positions himself against the tide of anti-Platonism. Johannes Thumfart (2008) helpfully indicates:

Badiou writes that today's most important political and theoretical values – Becoming (Nietzsche), Language (Wittgenstein), Sociality (Marx), Existence (Sartre), Process (Heidegger) and Political Pluralism (Popper) – can be identified by their differing forms of modern Anti-Platonisms.

The most influential inconsistency is probably the analytical philosophers' Anti-Platonism. Wittgenstein and Carnap especially attacked Plato because of his granting an eternal and unchangeable status to mathematical objects. Badiou notes that the analytical project of reducing all properties of mathematical and other objects of formal language to mere conventions is still to be debated and that the analytical philosophers too quickly eliminated any idealistic concept of language. The Anti-Platonism of analytical philosophy must, therefore, be re-thought (http://www.lacan.com/symptom/?p=64).

Badiou is also someone who has increasingly found himself surrounded by controversy: for his publication in 2005 of 'The Uses of the Word "Jew"'[3] and more recently for his *The Meaning of Sarkozy* (Badiou, 2008). He appeared recently on the BBC program HardTalk[4] where he was interviewed about his support for 'communism' replying that that the mere fact that the 'first attempts' to achieve communism 'failed' does not in any way amount to a proving of the idea itself to be false or in itself impossible to reach. Ramsey (2009) reviewing his interview positively taking Badiou's comment—'Never accept something as legitimate [just] because it is dominant'—as a starting point to suggest:

Badiou has done brilliant work exposing the contradictions, limitations, and hypocrisies that are embedded in dominant modes of contemporary thought, (including electoralism, liberal multiculturalism, and humanitarianism, including the discourse of human rights).[5]

While undoubtedly an important and influential philosopher and certainly one that also belongs in a special issue for this book, it is also the case that Badiou is written little on education. As Thomas Petersen and other contributors acknowledge it is only in the essay 'Art and Philosophy' from *Handbook of Inaesthetics*, that Badiou addresses education directly discussing the link between art and philosophy in terms of the 'pedagogical theme', which has collapsed. I shall not repeat the analysis better performed by the contributors except to note that Badiou declares 'the only education is an education *by truths*'. As A. J. Bartlett (2006: 53) comments, in this light Badiou invents a threefold analytical schema:

The didactic schema operates a pedagogy of surveillance, the romantic, a pedagogy of authentic identity as alienation, and the classical, a pedagogy of public service or state ethics. Thus, we can say, subtracting from Badiou's otherwise occupied assessment, that surveillance, identity, and ethics make up, the pedagogical forms inherent to the 'saturated' 20th century.

And he goes on to comment:

On Badiou's terms, education is that which makes the necessary arrangements for the manifestation of truths which are not opinions and which signify therefore the possibility for some other, new (political etc.) configuration. In fact using Badiou's analysis it is not going to [sic] far to claim that as our democracies are manifestations of the organized rule of opinion then the state system of education for which our democracies are responsible is without truth, without thought, and thus cannot operate other than as either 'oppressive or perverted' or indeed as both (p. 54).

Here is a trenchant critique of state education every bit as forceful as Freire's 'banking' concept and one that teaches us that to educate is to transform, as Barlett (2006) remarks:

Thus education amounts to either 'being' or, 'to have been' transformed. The questions, of course, are: by what, from what, to what? Is it by the state whose goal is perpetuation and whose method thereby is predicated on meiosistic repetition or, in Althusser's more 'structural' terms reproduction (of the relations of production)? Or is it by truths and thus to be transformed without predicate, educated without? (p. 58)

I am grateful to Kent den Heyer for organizing and editing this special and to him and his contributors for gracing the book with the work and analysis of Badiou's philosophy.

Notes

1. Photo credit is from the Faculty Page at the European Graduate School which lists his works including online works and also secondary sources at http://www.egs.edu/faculty/alain-badiou/biography/.
2. Badiou trained as a mathematician and he refers and uses Zermelo–Fraenkel set theory with the axiom of choice which is a standard axiomatic and foundation for mathematics, founded on a single primitive ontological notion namely that all individuals in the universe of discourse are sets. Axiom 9 is drawn from axioms 1–8 and is known as the 'axiom of choice' formulated by Ernst Zermelo in 1904 roughly to suggest that any collection of bins, each containing at least one object, it is possible to make a selection of exactly one object from each bin, even if there is an infinite number of bins and there is no 'rule' for which object to pick from each. See the entry on set theory by Thomas Jech (2002) at http://plato.stanford.edu/entries/set-theory/.

3. See http://www.lacan.com/badword.htm.
4. See http://video.google.com/videoplay?docid=7936414602517427743&ei=57uRSqzxM6PE2 wLBr6yuAw#.
5. See http://www.khukuritheory.net/j-ramsey-thoughts-on-badious-hardtalk-interview/.

References

Badiou, Alain (2004) 'Art and Philosophy' from *Handbook of Inaesthetics*, A. Toscano trans. (Stanford, Stanford University Press).
Badiou, Alain (2005) *Being and Event*, O. Feltham trans. (New York, Continuum).
Badiou, Alain (2008) *The Meaning of Sarkozy* (New York, Verso).
Bartlett, A. J. (2006) Conditional Notes on a New Republic, Cosmos and History, *The Journal of Natural and Social Philosophy*, 2: 1–2.
Ramsey, J. (2009) Thoughts on Badiou's HardTalk Interview, Khukuri: Toward a Radical Conception of Revolutionary Theory, at http://www.khukuritheory.net/j-ramsey-thoughts-on-badious-hardtalk-interview/.
Thumfart, Johannes (2008) Learning from Las Vegas, The Symptom 9, at http://www.lacan.com/symptom/?p=64.

Michael A. Peters
University of Illinois at Urbana-Champaign

1

Introduction: Alain Badiou: 'Becoming subject' to education

KENT DEN HEYER

Welcome to this book thinking education through the work of the French philosopher, Alain Badiou. Since 2000, the increased pace of translating Badiou's books written in the 1980s and '90s into English has created growing interest. Current attention suggests that Badiou will soon join Michael Foucault, Jacques Derrida and Emmanuel Levinas as another major French philosophical influence on Anglo-American scholarship (Gibson, 2006). Indeed, given the traffic in English translation of his work and the number of special issues attempting to come to terms with what his work might mean for a diverse range of scholarly fields—including this one, the first to examine Badiou in relation to education—we might say he has already arrived.

If Badiou has 'caught on' outside education, it might be explained by the 'affirmative' thrust of his thought that freshly affronts the doxa both of contemporary Anglo-American philosophy and more popular media-ated interpretations of the broader context within which we think. As part of his philosophical intervention into this present situation—and for Badiou all 'live thought' constitutes a militant's intervention—Badiou first describes contemporary philosophy—'hermeneutics' and 'post-modern' approaches being his favorite targets—as but a form of 'conservatism with a good conscience' (Badiou, 2001, p. 14). He asserts that the categories dominating contemporary philosophical work—of the Other, of difference, of language's trickster nature—lead either to a quasi-theology or observations of the obvious. In any case, and most importantly, Badiou argues that the categories of contemporary philosophy lack any ethical capacity to support people's potential to affirmatively invent 'the possibility of new possibilities' (Badiou, cf. in Cho & Lewis, 2005).

These claims are part of Badiou's broader project to re-think contemporary political subjectivity in an age he asserts is awash in a relativism on the one hand—in which every opinion is equal to every other—and run aground on an alleged 'end of history/Washington consensus' on the other in which each opinion is equally irrelevant to alter a situation dominated by political appeals to economic necessity. In support of people's capacities to affirmatively invent new realities, Badiou rehabilitates a concept of 'truths'. Let me briefly provide a brief overview of Badiou's work given better detail in each of this book's chapters.

For Badiou, 'truths' are not actualities to acquire, properties of interlocking social regimes, temporalized ideals or authenticities, derivable from moral precepts, or facts entrapped within any dialectic (Balibar, 2004). As he interprets, a 'truth'—or, rather, a generic 'truth-process'—is absent of pre-specified content (as articulated by any number of religious orders or present appeals for our necessity to believe in the 'free hand' of the Market) or destination (as with a 'scientific' Marxist interpretation of history). This interpretation of truth is also unrelated to any communitarian identification (e.g. race-thinking, nationalisms, gender, sexual orientations). Rather, truths consist of the material traces (i.e. in speech, art, and social movements) a 'becoming subject' produces in 'fidelity' to a singular 'truth-process' instigated by an 'event'. It is for these situated truth-processes that Badiou argues ethics and philosophy—and, as explored in this book, education—must lend support.

The status of an 'event' is, of course, a matter of much philosophical debate. Mariam Fraser (2006) writes that 'as a philosophical concept', an *event* 'exists in relation to a specific set of problems, including the problem of how to conceive of modes of individuation that pertain not to being, or to essences and representation, but to becoming and effectivity' (p. 129). Badiou links his interpretation of an 'event' to (one of his teachers) Lacan's 'void': at its most basic description, an event is an encounter with that which defies our symbolic apprehension. This encounter renders insufficient the 'opinions' that previously provided the taken-for-granted coordinates of our daily lives: a disturbance that creates the possibility of a truth-process that implicates us in that 'which cannot be calculated, predicted or managed' (Badiou, 2001, pp. 122–123; see Peter Taubman, this book).

Encountering this event, we confront the question of 'fidelity' which is precisely *the* question where ethics for Badiou begins: 'A crisis of fidelity is always what puts to the test, following the collapse of an image, the sole maxim of consistency (and thus ethics): Keep going!' (Badiou, 2001, p. 79). Badiou writes,

> I cannot, within the fidelity to fidelity that defines ethical consistency [of, and, to, a truth-process] take an interest in myself, and thus pursue my own interests. All my capacity for interest, which is my own perseverance in being, has *poured out* into the future consequences of the solution to this scientific problem, into the examination of the world in the light of love's being-two, into what I will make of my encounter, one night, with the eternal Hamlet, or into the next stage of the political process, once the gathering in front of the factory has dispersed. There is always only one question in the ethic of truths: how will I, as some-one, continue to exceed my own being? How will I link the things I know, in a consistent fashion, via the effects of being seized by the not-known? (Badiou, 2001, p. 50)

Encouraging this ethical maxim, Badiou warns against the 'Evil' (translated from his term in French, 'le Mal') made simultaneously possible only because of human potential to engage in the 'Good' of truth-processes.[1] For Badiou (2001), le Mal/ Evil comes in three derivatives: *simulacrum/terror*, or embracing a teleological fantasy of an existing situation's promised fulfillment (rather than the Lacanian 'void' at the heart of all situations); *betrayal*, which is to either to give up on a truth-process or to mistake one's truth-process for Truth; and *disaster*, when, mistaking the named content of a singular truth-process for Truth, Truth justifies the destruction of material conditions others require to engage their potential for truth-processes. These are the Evils to which the good of human potential for truth-processes potentially leads. Of course, both history and the present are full of examples where truth-inventions distort into 'disaster'. For Badiou, however, the relevant conclusion is not to deny the affirmative Good that is a truth, but to remain vigilant to the distortion of the Good that is le Mal.

As I note elsewhere, love provides the most poignant example of an 'event' that irrupts within (or, as Badiou describes it in several works, 'pierces' a hole in) the 'opinions' we assume define our situations (den Heyer, 2009). Love also exemplifies the simultaneously singular and universal quality of Badiou's affirmative ethics grounded in the particularities of situations.

All lovers—however unique the people and the circumstances—are 'becoming subject' to an event—falling in love—that is also universal in that love-as-'event' respects no pre-set rules or expectations, pre-existing identities or differences and, we must assume, is potentially available to all. In addition to other consequences, encountering an event such as love subtracts from what one thought to be the case of one's situation. This subtraction simultaneously creates the possibilities of a 'supplement' we enact in becoming more than the 'one' we thought (were 'opinion'-ated) we were (Badiou, 2001). In this case, we break with 'all previous fictional assemblages through which [we] organized [a] self-representation' (Badiou, 2001, p. 55).[2] In short, all lovers constitute a 'becoming subject' by embodying a 'disinterested interest' in inherited opinions and avoiding the Evil of an easy or expected resolution.

As with the case of love, the falling or event has past, and in passing, a hole remains, creating the condition for a collective subject to exercise a fidelity. In this sense, the proper verb tense with Badiou's use of an event and truth-process is neither the present nor the past, but rather the future anterior. In essence, a 'becoming subject'—faithful to the unpredictable implications of a truth event—declares 'this will have been true' pursuing exactly 'what it will be absurd *not* to have believed' (Gibson, 2006, p. 88: emphasis added). It is in this sense that Badiou borrows Lacan's concept of 'anticipatory certitude' as the militant engagement in a truth-process that is both the object and objective of his ethics (van Rompaey, 2006).

Given reasonable impressions to the contrary, and as explored more fully by contributors to this book, it is necessary to state that, for Badiou, a 'becoming subject' is a collective subjectivity entirely dependent on the emergence of an event. His is not a philosophical argument for Enlightened 'free will' or for an individualism that is fully in charge of itself. As with love, the unpredictable consequences of an 'event' mock such assertions. Further, rather than as a call for individual acts of heroism, his argument is more generously (and accurately, see Anna Strhan's contribution to this book) interpreted as a collective conviction to acting, speaking, and 'art-ing' (see jan jagodzinski, this book) that is always in a beholding relation to the event.

As Keith Jenkins (2004) notes, Badiou's ethic seeks to support a 'relativism of a certain kind' (p. 47). Like love, this relativism is based on the particularities of truth-processes and the concrete enactments of that process. Yet, however singular and particular a truth process, a truth-process must always proceed in the name of all; for 'when we abandon the universal [e.g. capacity to love], we have universal horror [i.e. expressions of hate] (Badiou, cf. in Hallward, 2000). Badiou's 'relativism [of truth processes emergent from particular situations] of a certain kind [that proceed in the name of all—"differences then are precisely what truths depose, or render insignificant"]' offers educators a potentially powerful guide to re-vivify our purposes for teaching and learning in the present historical situation. For example, while it is as possible to plan an event as it is to schedule when one falls in love, can teachers translate a vision of Badiou's ethics into curricular arrangements? In what ways might educators take up Badiou's notion of truth-process to work for educational standards that reflect our higher affirmative potentials (den Heyer, 2009b)?

Taking this kind of question as a starting point, Anna Strhan's contribution to this book deploys several key concepts from Badiou to contest the poverty of vision about human potential expressed in an education dominated by 'economic managerialism'. This economic logic she explores turns institutionalized education (and all involved) into the poor abstracted equivalences of a deterritorialized currency devoid of the richness of human and contextual particularities. Strhan further explores the inadequate response to this situation by Marxist derived critical theory.

Strhan writes that such critique actually supports 'the count of the market', conceiving that any education problem 'can [be] rectified by *proper* economic distributions and recognitions'. In her reading, economic managerialism within education and its 'critique' from critical theory constitute a mutually reinforcing part of our contemporary situation; not unlike 'post' discourses that often in effect support—rather than adequately propose anything other than—a teetering 'modernity'.

As with Strhan, all scholars in this book wrestle with Badiou's philosophical demand and its potential implication for a more proactive arrangement of knowledge in schools organized to instigate truth-processes that might supplement inherited commitments (den Heyer, 2009b). Indeed, this very concern centrally animates the contribution by Kathleen R. Kesson and James G. Henderson.

Starting with the affirmation of teachers as curriculum decision-makers, their chapter exemplifies the practice of eclectic theorizing they propose educators to take up so as to engage the humanly-enriching complexities of teaching-learning. They link Badiou and the affirmative thrust of his philosophy and ethics to prominent US curriculum scholars such as John Dewy, Maxine Greene, Eliot Eisner, and William F. Pinar.

For example, to Pinar's (2007) recent formulations of curriculum study as 'disciplinarity'—which includes a *vertical* dimension referring to 'the intellectual history of the discipline' (Pinar, 2007, p. xiii) and a *horizontal* dimension consisting of interpreting the impacting conditions of a contemporary intellectual, social, and political milieu—Kesson and Henderson add 'diagonality'. As they interpret, dia-gonality 'represents the journey of a courageous and experimental educator, with a mindset capable of embracing paradox, rupture, and uncertainty ... as well as an inclination toward the critical self-examination that lies at the heart of democratic ethical fidelity in education'. Such a fidelity, they suggest, requires a teacher capacity to be less certain and more comfortable with our ontological reality 'constituted by an infinite set of elements ... In effect, from an ontological point of view, [teachers] have no choice' but to embrace uncertainty in their work of artistic inquiry and potential for truth-processes. As articulated by Kesson and Henderson, Badiou presents us with a difficult demand.

Badiou's demand is absent of content or means. He provides us only with an mathematically-derived ontological reading of infinity—within which we identify ourselves with the sub-sets the situation provides and requires in order to continue to exist (whether a sub-set defined by race, sexual orientation etc)—and a philosophical exhortation to 'continue to exceed ourselves' even as we face the unpredictable consequences certain to come.

In this demand, Badiou's thought resonates with the psychoanalytical insights explored by Shoshona Felman (1987) and the 'impossibility of teaching:' 'in one way or another every pedagogy stems from its confrontation with the impossibility of teaching' (Felman, 1987, p. 72). What fresh readings does Badiou's work offer psychoanalytical theorizations of an education that presumes a steady subject and a singular subjectivity? This question is central to the contribution here by Peter Taubman.

Specifically, in his typically inviting style of expression, Taubman asks what dangers are inherent in Badiou's 'event'-ual ethics? What distinguishes an event as 9/11 might be interpreted to have been for the Bush Administration from an event with less bloody consequences for others who suffer a fidelity by Bush *et al.* to that event? Readers will benefit from Taubman's consideration of what to take and what to take with great caution from Badiou's formulation of ethics. Taubman reads Badiou to explore an ethic of teaching that subjectively engages with the desires that, in part, constitute our shared relationality and the Lacanian Real that underwrites such. jagodzinski too takes up Badiou through Lacan (among other influential French scholars) but directs our attention to their implications in regards to 'art-ing' and art education.

jagodzinski reads Badiou's articulation of *inaesthetics* through Lacan's three registers (Real, Symbolic, Imaginary) and the work of Gilles Deleuze and Jacques Rancière. He relates these thinkers to explore the ways in which 'art cannot be taught', but can, however, 'educate!' Along the way, jagodzinski provides grateful readers with examples of art that both provide material reference to Badiou's intellectual oeuvre and point to its lacunae. These consist of five problems explored by jagodzinski as impacting both Badiou's theorization of art and its theoretical implications for education. In this regard, jagodzinski offers readers a depth of technical engagement with Badiou that escapes introductory enunciations. Among other insights he provides is an invention of a term I hope continues to receive consideration in talk about education: 'I have been using the term self-refleXive as opposed to self-reflection or self-reflexivity, to get at the "X" referring to the fidelity of the event itself'.

In a resonate exploration to that of jagodzinski, Thomas Peterson takes up art education related to the teaching, learning, and living of poetry. Examining Badiou's claim that poetry is a vehicle for truths, Peterson challenges poetry's educated domestication; a domestication he labels as a 'liberal' orthodoxy that denies any relevance to either the event or truth as referenced by jagodzinski's 'X'. Rather, in contemporary education, students are directed to take apart a poem to reveal its author's psychological dimensions or intentions or to connect it as an instance of this or that movement. As Peterson details, such direction is not only empirical questionable, but constitutes an evasion of humanity's potential '... to aspire to the Immortal' of which poetry constitutes a material trace. Rejecting contemporary enactments of liberalism (in schools and beyond), Peterson arrives at the conclusion that 'a truth-process requires that teacher and student come together as a unified subject involved in an active and transitive confrontation with past knowledge'. With similar concern, Charles Barbour organizes his contribution around the question of whether—and to what extent—education can become a space of love, science, art, or politics where a truth might break through?

Barbour leans up against each other the work of Badiou with his contemporary, compatriot, and sometime philosophical foe, Rancière. While jagodzinski emphasizes the aesthetic site of disagreement between Badiou and Rancière, Barbour highlights their thought regarding the more commonly recognized political field. While they offer distinct lines of thought regarding the role of aesthetic sensibilities in politics, Barbour explores a shared axiomatic quality to their work. As he details, both Rancière and Badiou can be reasonably summarized as writing in defense of people's capacity to willfully exercise their own intelligence (Rancière, 1991) and potential for becoming subject to their own truth-processes (Badiou, 2001) independently of both institutionalized life and curricular plans. In short, both work from an 'axiom of equality'.

As Barbour cites Badiou to note, equality 'must be *postulated* not *willed*'. Genuine political action involves 'not the desire for equality, but the consequence of its axiom' (Badiou, 2005, p. 112). Barbour writes, 'equality can be neither planned nor accomplished. It can only be practiced, and through this practice verified. It can only be practiced if it is axiomatically assumed. And conversely, it can never be practiced if it is axiomatically denied'. In articulating this quality of axiomatic equality shared by Rancière and Badiou and its potential consequences with verve, Barbour lays the groundwork for thinking through an education premised on equality rather than a project allegedly seeking such.[3]

As with Barbour, the work of all scholars collected here express an evident commitment to a vision of education as a space where people come together to work out not only what is possible, but also to explore 'precisely that which, from within the situation, is declared to be impossible ... an event-ality still suspended from its name' (Badiou, 2001, pp. 121/126). These scholars also provide readers who may be coming freshly to Badiou with a sense both of the resonance and disjuncture between his oeuvre and those thinkers more familiar to the audience of this book. For this they are to be commended. Likewise, I would also like to thank Michael Peters for his willingness to create the space for this book to exist. To all, 'keep going'!

Notes

1. It is important to emphasize that, in the French, 'le Mal', connotes sickness in addition to something very bad and thus invokes shades of Lacan and Foucaultian analyses into human situations. Evil, however, is a tactically useful translation in my opinion in that it secularizes the term as a question of ethics and human situations rather than morality and derived rules of right and wrong from hole/ly texts. I wish to thank Jim Henderson for pointing me towards the implications of this translation.
2. Tangentially, this notion of 'fictional assemblages' provides a wonderful description of curriculum as relates to history and schooling more generally.
3. I would like to thank Charles Barbour. With great generosity of spirit, he was the first to introduce me to the work of Badiou which then set this and other projects in motion.

References

Badiou, A. (2001) *Ethics: An essay on the understanding of evil*, P. Hallward, trans. (London, Verso).

Badiou, A. (2005) *Handbook of Inaesthetics*, A. Toscano, trans. (Stanford, CA, Stanford University Press).

Balibar, E. (2004) The History of Truth: Alain Badiou in French philosophy, in: P. Hallward (ed.), *Think Again: Alain Badiou and the future of philosophy* (London, Continuum), pp. 21–88.

Cho, D. & Lewis, T. (2005) Education and Event: Thinking radical pedagogy in the era of standardization, *Studies in Media & Information Library Education*, 5:2. http://utpress. utoronto.ca/journal/ejournals/simile (accessed September 21, 2008).

den Heyer, K. (2009) What if Curriculum (of a Certain Kind) Doesn't Matter? *Curriculum Inquiry*, 39:1, pp. 27–40.

den Heyer, K. (2009b) Education as an Affirmative Invention: Alain Badiou and the purpose of teaching and curriculum, *Educational Theory*, 59:4, pp. 441–63.

Felman, S. (1987) *Jacques Lacan and the Adventure of Insight: Psychoanalysis in contemporary culture* (Cambridge, MA, Harvard University Press).

Fraser, M. (2006) Event, *Theory Culture & Society*, 23, pp. 129–32.

Gibson, A. (2006) *Beckett and Badiou: The pathos of intermittency* (Oxford, New York, Oxford University Press).

Hallward, P. (2000) Ethics without Others: A reply to Critchley on Badiou's Ethics, *Radical Philosophy*, 102:July/August, pp. 27–30.

Jenkins, K. (2004) Ethical Responsibility and the Historian: On the possible end of a history 'of a certain kind, *History and Theory, Theme Issue*, 43, pp. 43–60.

Pinar, W. F. (2007) *Intellectual Advancement Through Disciplinarity: Verticality and horizontality in curriculum studies* (Rotterdam, Sense Publishers).

Rancière, J. (1991) *The Ignorant School Master: Five lessons in intellectual emancipation*, K. Ross, trans. (Stanford, CA, Stanford University Press).

van Rompaey, C. (2006) A question of fidelity, *Cosmos and History: The Journal of Natural and Social Philosophy*, 2:1–2, pp. 350–58.

2
Badiou, Pedagogy and the Arts

Thomas E. Peterson

Art is pedagogical for the simple reason that it produces truths and because 'education' (save in its oppressive or perverted expressions) has never meant anything but this: to arrange the forms of knowledge in such a way that some truth may come to pierce a hole in them. (Badiou, 2005b, p. 9)

Introduction

Though Badiou has rarely discussed the topic of education, he has constantly been involved in the assessment of knowledge and truth within the current academic and intellectual culture of the West. The breadth and depth of Badiou's work is forbidding, and yet the topical nature of so much of it makes the French philosopher an irresistible source of insights for those seeking to reshape and reform current pedagogical concepts and practices. In this chapter I follow the implicit itinerary of Badiou's thought on pedagogical matters, focusing in particular on the inter-relationship between the academic disciplines and Badiou's conviction that truths are manifest diversely in diverse areas of endeavor, especially the four conditions he labels as art, politics, love and science. Related to the epigraph above, I seek to answer the following questions: What are the 'oppressive or perverted expressions' of education today and where do we find them? How does arts education, with its demands for an intrinsic truth-seeking method represent a paradigm for instruction across the disciplines? Throughout my exploration of these questions, I will call on the pedagogical implications of Badiou's interpretation of ethics.

With respect to the first question, Badiou tends to locate the misguided expressions of education in contemporary liberalism in the broad social plane; these expressions are evident in the classroom and curriculum, and in the larger structures of the academy. To illustrate this we will summarize Badiou's critique of current aesthetics and its tendency to bracket the truth of the work of art. This bracketing is found in the customary didactic methods for analyzing a poem that tend to fixate on the contours of the *self*, that is on the subjectivity of the poet which the reader analyzes and interprets for the sake of a psychological identification. I will also contrast Badiou's 'ethic of truths' with the 'ethics of necessity' found in the contemporary political culture of 'consensus'. In Badiou's view, the culture of consensus harmfully reduces education to the dissemination of knowledge and thereby forecloses possibilities of truth-processes. If, as Bill Readings demonstrates, today's university has drifted away from the Humboldtian model—with its emphasis on the integration of 'objective science (cultural knowledge) with subjective spiritual and moral training (cultivation)' (Readings, 1996, p. 66)—and toward a corporate and entrepreneurial model, what Badiou provides is a kind of clinical study of the character, motivations and symptomology of this mutation. The scope of this mutation is hinted at by empirical studies that show how today's research universities are 'shifting from a public good knowledge/learning regime to an academic capitalist knowledge/learning regime' (Slaughter & Rhoades, 2004, p. 7).

Our discussion of the first question—that is of Badiou's critique of ethical and organizational matters—will prepare the ground for a discussion of the second question, regarding the intrinsic nature of arts education. It is Badiou's conviction that the relationship between art and philosophy implicates a third element: the education of the subject. This subject emerges in the process of witnessing a truth or, in more Badiouian terms, becomes instantiated as the possible result of an event to which the subject then remains faithful. As such, this education of the subject constitutes a break with established knowledge. After a summary of Badiou's three-part understanding of the truth-process, I refer to his discussions of selected modern poets (Mallarmé, Perse) as examples of one way to interpret the pedagogical implications of his philosophy and ethics. Viewed as nomadic figures and truth-seekers, the poets serve to exemplify the importance of those traits for educators as well. I pursue this complex notion in a discussion of Badiou's book on St. Paul. Badiou sees in Paul and specifically the apostle's subjectivity, a teacher and divulgator of Christianity who serves as Badiou's exemplar to explicate Badiou's interpretation of a truth-process and an ethics of truth.

Thus, the contours of this chapter proceed from the more external framing of the educational situation—whose basis is that of the human animal in pursuit of its self-interest and the standard pedagogue disseminating the encyclopedia of knowledge—to the nature of truth-process. I arrive at the conclusion that a truth-process requires that teacher and student come together as a unified subject involved in an active and transitive confrontation with past knowledge. While the uncertainty and risk of this process cannot be overlooked, the new knowledge that results from one's investigations is itself a positive reward and life-changing confirmation of the need to reject the inert opinions of static knowledge and to invest in a process of learning that is at once passionate and ethical.

21st Century Ethics and the Problem of Evil

Badiou defines modernity by asking questions. His interrogative style helps to make his philosophy comprehensible to the non-specialist. This is certainly true for his assessments of our current intellectual milieu, as we look back on the 20th century. In addition to the great human tragedies visited on that century, Badiou asks if the major critical schools of thought that characterized it were able to keep pace with the great advances and volatility in the arts. He concludes that they did not: 'The century that is coming to a close was characterized by the fact that it did not introduce, on a massive scale, any new schema' (Badiou, 2005b, p. 5). The three singular systems of thought that emerged in the 20th century had severe limitations in addressing the work of art: 'It is clear that as regards the thinking of art, Marxism is didactic, psychoanalysis classical, and Heideggerian hermeneutics romantic' (Badiou, 2005b, p. 5). While not introducing new schemes, or a new relationship between art and philosophy, the 20th century 'experienced the *saturation*' (2005b, p. 7) of the earlier doctrines. Given this state of affairs, none of the doctrines—didacticism, classicism, romanticism—retained its vitality. What resulted was a 'desperate "disrelation" between art and philosophy, together with the pure and simple collapse of what had circulated between them: the pedagogical theme' (Badiou, 2005b, p. 7). Thus it is a profoundly pedagogical motivation that leads Badiou to ask the following questions about the 'immanence' and 'singularity' of the work of art:

> 'Immanence' refers to the following question: Is truth really internal to the artistic effect of works of art? Or is the artwork instead nothing but in the instrument of the external truth? 'Singularity' points us to another question: Does the truth testified by art belong to it absolutely? Or can this truth circulate among other registers of work-producing thought? (Badiou, 2005b, p. 9)

While the above doctrines continue to be relevant, they offer the teacher only partial and indirect means of assessing the artifact; in contrast, the event-based (or 'evental') scheme deals with the art work both in terms of its immanence and its singularity. It is Badiou's conviction that the arts produce their own truths; these are 'processes' and 'productions' more than 'illuminations' or discoveries of something preexistent. The pursuit of truth—which coincides with the fidelity to the 'Immortal' within oneself—is integral to a positive ethics. It makes no sense to discuss this ethics in general terms insofar as ethics arises only within particular situations: 'There is only the *ethic-of* (of politics, of love, of science, of art)' (Badiou, 2002, p. 28).

Unfortunately there is a widespread tendency to invoke ethics as an end in itself; this end is arrived at by means of 'consensus' and in the name of such ideas as 'otherness', 'human rights' and 'democracy'. The problem with such seemingly valid causes is that they are used to supplant and ignore the realities of concrete situations: 'The reign of ethics is one symptom of a universe ruled by a distinctive combination of resignation in the face of necessity together with a purely negative, if not destructive, will. It is this combination that should be designated as nihilism' (Badiou, 2002, p. 30). The 'ethics of human rights' is in fact a laissez-faire liberalism that enforces the passivity of the citizen:

> What is being inflicted on us today ... is the conviction that the will, dominated by a suffocating reality principle whose distillate is the economy, should behave with extraordinary circumspection—lest it expose the world to grave disasters. There is a 'nature of things' and violence must not be done to it. Basically, the spontaneous philosophy of our 'modernizing' propaganda is Aristotelian: Let the nature of things

manifest its proper ends. We must not do, but be: laissez-faire. (Badiou, 2007, p. 99)

The ideological control of the subject is reflected in an adulteration during the 20th century of the ideals of the French Revolution; to begin with, genuine freedom has been 'reviled' and replaced by a purely formal idea of freedom:

> 'Formal freedom' means a freedom that is neither articulated to a global egalitarian project nor practised subjectively as fraternity.
>
> Throughout the century, equality is the strategic goal ... Freedom, as the unlimited power of the negative, is presupposed, but not thematized. As for fraternity, it is the real itself pure and simple, the sole subjective guarantee of the novelty of experiences, since equality remains programmatic and liberty instrumental. (2007, p. 101)

Such liberalism is based on the unexamined premise of democracy, and yields in practice to an 'anything goes' mixture of relativism. Anthony Wilden has summarized this brand of thinking as follows:

> For the classic liberal, the quantum-relativistic theory had three useful political translations and one conjuring trick:
> • Everyone is an individual atom separated from every other.
> • Everyone is equal.
> • Everything is relative to everything else.
> • Both-and is either/or (or vice versa).
> The basic structure of the liberal ideology rests on the illiberal belief that there are 'two sides to every question'—and no real hierarchies of power, where the questioner has the power and the authority to harm the person or family or other treasured relations of the one under interrogation.
>
> By its very structure capitalist liberal theory (born in the English Revolution of 1642–88) ignores the fact that many questions have many 'sides' (religion is the best example); that certain questions and kinds of questions—such as racism and torture—have only one side; and that other problems can't be defined by the word 'sides' at all, since they don't have any to start with. (Wilden, 1987, p. 305)

The liberal thinking impugned by Wilden fails to discern between 'analytic logic' ('a single level and static logic, outside time and change') and 'dialectical logic' ('a many-leveled and dynamic logic, within time and dependent—like learning—on duration') (Wilden, 1987, p. 277). Drawing on such modern discoveries as Einstein's theory of relativity and Heisenberg's uncertainty principle, social scientists and others applied the notion of relativism indiscriminately, ignoring in the process the hierarchical structures of living systems or the interdependencies of the academic disciplines.

It is precisely this brand of liberal thinking that is critiqued by Roland Barthes as 'neither-nor-ism' in his published lecture course on 'The Neutral', where we read:

> *... neither-norism: nothing radical in it, a mere social (even, in our contexts, professional) tactic: self-serving expression of a political position = rhetoric (persuasion) of this position —> rhetoric of the neither-nor wavering (myth of the scale, instrument of measure {justesse}): but the neither-norish wavering leaves a remainder: underneath the neither-nor rhetoric, there ends up being a choice —> great media provider of the neither-nor rhetoric:* Le Monde: *perpetually weighing pros and cons ...* (Barthes, 2005, p. 80)

Such thinking has trivialized humanism's historical focus on the universal in a way that is symmetrical with the antimodernist scholarship of the older, more elitist and hieratic, form of humanism.[1] One has seen in this regard a conflation between the economic theory of free trade known as liberalism (or neo-liberalism) and the liberal philosophy oriented toward the freedom of the individual to be but not to act. What has largely been ignored is the nobility of liberal learning in the Senecan sense. As Martha Nussbaum notes, it was Seneca who conceived of citizenship as being based on a freedom that does not derive from social class, but from intellectual autonomy and respect. This Senecan liberality depends on the awareness of one's smallness in the larger scheme of things, of the immensity of one's unknowing. As such it fosters humility and respect for the differences of others.[2] If one is to reject the laissez-faire type of liberalism—which reaffirms the closed values of the aristocracy—then the Socratic method must be employed, also in stating curricular goals and institutional exigencies. Teachers like Badiou who employ the Socratic method encourage a class-blind cosmopolitanism, challenging students to represent their positions and their histories.

It is arguable that one of the tangible results of neo-liberalism on the academic campus has been the wide-scale introduction of courses in non-traditional areas over the last thirty years. As Edward Said has stated, the focus on values and truth of a properly construed humanism has been absent from a host of disciplinary approaches born out of the post-Vietnam War period's pursuit of social and personal relevance: area studies, feminism, post-colonial studies, post-structuralism and post-modernism. Said makes the point that the purported humanists have abandoned or trivialized humanism's historical focus on universality by adopting anti-foundationalist identity politics and theory-laden postmodernist stances. Said suggests that the 'radically multicultural' nature of United States culture demands that one invest such area studies as listed above with the same pursuit of universals and the same passion for philology that one would expect in the traditional curriculum. Said argues that we find ourselves beset with:

> ... antifoundationalism, discourse analysis, automatized and tokenized relativism, and professionalism, among other orthodoxies ... . The alternatives seem now to be quite impoverishing: either become a technocratic deconstructionist, discourse analyst, new historicist, and so on, or retreat into a nostalgic celebration of some past state of glory associated with what is sentimentally evoked as humanism. What is missing altogether is some intellectual, as opposed to a merely technical,

component to humanistic practice that might restore it to a place of relevance in our time. (Said, 2000, p. 70)

The liberalism exposed by the above scholars, like the ethics of necessity denounced by Badiou, represents the evasion of humanity's potential to rise above the goals of mere communitarian identifications and self-interest and to aspire to the 'Immortal'. It is Badiou's insight to note that this ethics is founded on the claim of Evil's a priori existence in the world. Evil indeed exists (as it does in Badiou's ethics), but only by virtue of the existence of the Good. On a concrete level, Badiou sees the ethics of human rights as a means to preserve the status quo and resist 'the way towards the Good as the superhumanity of humanity, towards the Immortal as the master of time' (Badiou, 2002, p. 32). As such, this ethics is the public relations arm of the individualism and profit-driven self-interest of the age: 'today we endure the dominance of an artificial individualism: ... the relation of money, the relation to economic and social success, the relation to sex' (Badiou, 2007, p. 98). Since Evil (such as barbarism, terrorism) precedes Good in this doctrine, human rights are construed as the rights to be free of Evil.

Badiou is not naïve about the consequences of resistance. The affirmation of the Good can lead one to a fundamentally asocial existence (which is not to say that one lives as a recluse or an ascetic: these are but simulacra for the lifestyle of commitment). For to affirm the Good, and avoid the Evil possible because of the Good, is to confront the Immortal in oneself with such fidelity that one's encounters with others exceed the boundaries of conventional sociability; conversely, one must '[reject] the idea of a consensual or a priori recognition of Evil' (Badiou, 2002, p. 61): 'For if our only agenda is an ethical engagement against an Evil we recognize a priori, how are we to envisage any transformation of the way things are?' (Badiou, 2002, p. 14). Viewed in this perverted way, Evil can only be one of three things: 'the betrayal in oneself of the Immortal that you are'; 'to identify truth with total power'; or 'to believe that an event convokes not the void of the earlier situation, but its plenitude' (Badiou, 2002, p. 71). These are the Evils that must be resisted by those who would pursue the truth, a pursuit undertaken from the 'perspective of the Good' (Badiou, 2002, p. 67).

At heart, says Badiou, this individualism is driven by the forces of self-interest and competition. In this ethic of human rights, humanity is abased to the animal plane, thus lowering the human being to status of potential victim. What is elided in 'Ethics as the avoidance of Evil' is the vision of man the Immortal, the human being who, by the force of thought, resists this abasement to the status of victim. By essentially designing a split between two groups—'On the side of the victims, the haggard animal exposed on television screens. On the side of the benefactors, conscience and the imperative to intervene' (Badiou, 2002, p. 13)—the supporters of 'human rights' have neglected the political reality that underlies the suffering of the Third World; in this way they have unwittingly devised the ideology of a self-damning western Man who forbids himself 'to imagine the Good, to devote his collective powers to it' (Badiou, 2002, p. 14). The implications for a philosophy of education are clear; whether one's field is the humanities or social sciences, the physical sciences, life sciences or the arts, the impact of a cultural relativism based on the suppression of thought aimed at puncturing a hole in knowledge with new truths is lethal. If 'every truth is the coming-to-be of that which is not' (Badiou, 2002, p. 27), the current intellectual regime resists any such radical change in the name of a constituted knowledge that is by its very nature static and fatalistic.

In summary, for Badiou the collapse of progressive movements aimed at social revolution left a gap among intellectuals that was filled by the 'human rights' and 'ethics' movements, attempts at self-legitimation that endorsed the credo of individualism or communal identities over any 'politics of collective liberation' (Badiou, 2002, p. 5). Such a status quo simply ignores the material realities and concrete situations of the world that are beyond the privileged purview of liberalism.

The Ontological Interdependency of the Arts and Sciences

It has been widely observed that in today's academy the disciplines of the arts and sciences have grown more disparate; that niche-research tends to prevail over more integrated pursuits; and that the humanities have fallen under the aegis of postmodernity, a direction that asserts the end of metaphysics, the collapse of the foundations of thought, and the false hope of any conceptualization of truths. Badiou has argued against this knowledge-regime. By rejecting the particularistic and identitarian cultivation of knowledge, he has defended the universalist pursuit of the truth and connected it to the discreteness and operational interdependency of the arts and sciences; that is to say, he has rejected the notion of philosophy as *primus inter pares* [first among equals]. By investigating the tensions that exist at the boundaries of philosophy—especially its boundaries with poetry and mathematics—he has distinguished those fields both in terms of their autonomous operational languages and their respective mutualities. By articulating the need for philosophers to stand-down and trim their sails, Badiou has stressed the truth-mission of the arts and the critical role of mathematics in defining a liberating ontology.

Philosophy and mathematics share the mode of *dianoia*, 'the thought that traverses, the thought that links and deduces' (Badiou, 2005b, p. 17). The difference in their pursuit of objectivity is reflected by the difference in their approach to being. While philosophy can only approximate or make general statements about truths, mathematics 'thinks the configurations of multiple-being directly' (Badiou, 2005b, p. 20). Unlike either philosophy or mathematics, poetry depends on 'the immediate singularity of experience' (Badiou, 2005b, p. 18). Poetry 'forbids' *dianoia*: 'the poem is a thought that cannot be discerned or separated as a thought' (Badiou, 2005b, pp. 18, 19). The great poems cannot be paraphrased, but are their own most economic statement. As such, poetry possesses 'an ethic of mystery' and expresses the power of language; this power constitutes the 'unnamable' of poetry just as for mathematics the unnamable is found in its 'consistency' (Badiou, 2005b, p. 23).

This feature of mathematics is seen in Gödel's theorem: 'it is impossible for a mathematical formalism ... to contain a demonstration of its own consistency' (Badiou, 2007, p. 163). In other words, rather than seeing this presence of an unresolved 'trace' element in the mathematical formalization as requiring a return to hermeneutics, Badiou asks what Gödel himself saw as the implications of his 'dem-onstrations': 'He sees in them a lesson of infinity, as well as the ransom of ignorance that must be paid every time knowledge is extorted from the real: to partake in a truth is also to measure that other truths exist, truths that we do not yet partake in' (Badiou, 2007, pp. 163–4). Badiou sees the role of mathematics as pivotal to a rever-sal of the excesses of postmodernity on the one hand and analytic philosophy on the other. Pronouncing himself against 'the disastrous consequences of philosophy's "lin-guistic turn" ' (Badiou, 2004, pp. 16–17), Badiou notes how practitioners of this 'turn' have ignored the matheme as 'a condition for philosophy' (Badiou, 2004, p. 21). Similarly, analytical philosophers, who have been faithful to the logic of the matheme, have not endorsed poetry: 'One of the peculiar characteristics of my own project is that it requires both the reference to poetry and a basis in mathematics' (Badiou, 2004, p. xv). Just as Badiou distinguishes the role of the matheme from the work of philosophy, he also asserts the autonomy of poetry and the arts, freeing them from their subjection to philosophy. The steps of poets 'to desuture philosophy and poetry' has the effect of liberating both practices from any 'rivalry' and moves beyond the Heideggerian 'sermon of the end of philosophy' (Badiou, 2003a, p. 98).

Throughout his work, Badiou exploits a discursive modality that exploits the possibility of dialogue between thinkers in diverse disciplines or historical backgrounds. Badiou often juxtaposes the voices of distant authors, positing the points of an imaginary debate. In doing so he explores the connections between philosophy, literature and science, distilling the positions of thinkers who have too often been dispatched to separate floors of the ideal library, never to meet. Thus in an anti-Platonic era such as our own, Badiou re-introduces Platonism as compatible with a transdisciplinary ontology. It is critical that such ontology engage the discoveries of the past in a way that is not deterministic or finite so as to welcome new and emerging forms of knowledge and new systems of classification. As Badiou writes in the introduction to *Theoretical Writings*, 'In order for the theoretical triad of being, truth, and subject to hold, it is necessary to think the triad that follows from it—which is to say the triad of the multiple (along with the void), the event (along with its site) and the generic (along with the new forms of knowledge which it allows us to force)' (Badiou, 2004, p. xv).

Badiou's theories are refreshing at a time when the humanistic and social sciences curriculums are weighted down by area studies courses overly concerned with the assertion of oppositions or of truth as a property belonging to a social group; when research funding can be influenced overly by earmarks or protocols established by non-experts concerning the desirability of certain results over others; and when scientific discoveries that do not conform to the agendas of governments are met with denialism.

The name 'culture' comes to obliterate that of 'art'. The word 'technology' obliterates the word 'science'. The word 'management' obliterates the word 'politics'. The word 'sexuality' obliterates love. The 'culture-technology-management-sexuality' system, which has the immense merit of being homogeneous to the market, and all of whose terms designate a category of commercial presentation, constitutes the modern nominal occlusion of the 'art-science-politics-love' system, which identifies truth procedures typologically. (Badiou, 2003b, p. 12)

Insofar as the educational profession is committed, in principle, to the pursuit of the truth, the 'occlusion' Badiou speaks of has dire consequences. Insofar as language is the life-blood of the educator, when language is distorted (as seen in the above citation) what emerges is an ersatz institutional life. The inherent modesty of the arts in the overall curriculum has not held up well under the weight of new commercial demands on the learning 'product', while funds for art programs in schools have been slashed. As Martha Nussbaum suggests in her chapter 'Compassion and Public Life', students not instructed in the arts fail to acquire empathy and compassion and even tend to exhibit a 'pathological narcissism' (Nussbaum, 2001, p. 432).

Teaching the Universal: The Model of St. Paul

St. Paul is considered by Badiou to be a nomadic militant, 'a poet-thinker of the event'. The event is the death and resurrection of Jesus Christ, but in the teaching of the universalist consequences of the event, Paul scrupulously avoids a defense of Christianity based on miracles, wisdom or prophecy. He rejects the centrality of suffering and victimage to the event, and dismisses as irrelevant *avant la lettre* any Christian philosophy. Paul bases his doctrine—'Paul's epistles are the only truly *doctrinal* texts in the New Testament' (2003b, p. 33)—on the conviction of the resurrection, on the requirement that each Christian experience resurrection, and on the weakness of the individual subject when confronting the force of truth. What Badiou's analysis of St. Paul arrives at is its validity for non-Christians as well as Christians: 'If Paul helps us to seize the link between eventual grace and the universality of the True, it is so that we can tear the lexicon of grace and encounter away from its religious confinement' (2003b, p. 66).

Specifically, the didactic and instructive figure of St. Paul is examined in terms of his '[investigation of a] law capable of structuring a subject devoid of all identity and suspended to an event whose only "proof" lies precisely in its having been declared by a subject' (2003b, p. 5). Badiou—who labels the event in question, Christ's resurrection, a 'fable'—argues that the objective truth of the event is not at issue in discussing the achievement of Paul's universalism, the merit of which was to have separated the 'truth procedure from the cultural "historicity" wherein opinion presumes to dissolve it' (Badiou, 2003b, p. 6). By so doing, Paul returned the truth-procedure to the universal subject who is not identified with particular cultural traits or origins. Paul's teachings do not repeat the parables and sayings of Christ, since he knows that Christianity's spread will not depend on such particular and contingent, anecdotal or historical evidence. Instead, '[the] paradoxical connection between a subject without identity and a law without support provides the foundation for the possibility of a universal teaching within history itself' (Badiou, 2003b, p. 5). It is this elevation of teaching that distances Paul from the 'culturalist ideology and the "victimist" conception of man' (Badiou, 2003b, p. 6). According to Badiou, the same ideologies of power and wisdom, and the same victimism, that permeated Paul's society are common today: we are beset by 'cultural and historical relativism that today constitutes at once a topic of public opinion, a "political" motivation, and a framework for research in the human sciences' (Badiou, 2003b, p. 6). This corrupt educational framework is tied to the 'identitarian logic' that separates out different ethnic or religious groups for different applications of the law. Just as Paul writes, 'There is neither Jew nor Greek, there is neither slave nor free, there is neither male nor female' (Galatians 3.28), Badiou insists that for any inquiry into the truth to succeed, 'the identitarian and communitarian categories ... must be *absented* from the process, failing which no truth has the slightest chance of establishing its persistence and accruing its immanent infinity' (Badiou, 2003b, pp. 9, 11).

Paul is the antidialectician, the believer in faith's power over the law, who can still bring the Gentiles under the legal auspices of the Judeo-Christian membership; and he is the believer in grace who can persuade the Judeo-Christian priesthood to accept the equality of the Gentiles. Paul is not attached to Jerusalem as center of Christianity, but is a nomad, similar in this regard to the great poets of the 19th and 20th centuries, who, as I explore later, opposed the exclusion of others from their community on the basis of identitarian or nationalistic categories. As an educator, Paul is maieutic, intervening in the life of the reader as he did in the lives of those remote Christian communities he visited. He is focused on the educational process and production, not on the replication of a system or the experience of the ineffable. Badiou compares him in this regard to modern thinkers like Lacan and Wittgenstein, whose texts are interventions and not systematic treatises: 'Like Lacan, who considers analytical discourse only in order to inscribe it within a mobile schema wherein it is connected to the discourses of the master, the hysteric, and the university, Paul institutes "Christian discourse" only by distinguishing its operations from those of Jewish discourse and Greek discourse' (Badiou, 2003b, p. 41).

Applying Paul to our current educational scenario in the West emphasizes that truth is not knowledge and must not be collapsed into it. As our educational institutions mechanically perfect themselves to be transmitters of knowledge, equipped with the most advanced technologies, discussions of truth are marginalized as too personal or simply too resistant to quantitative assessment. Or the (simulacrum of) truth is deemed to 'belong' to one of the identitarian and particularist categories that have flooded the curriculum.

In contrast, the figure of Paul is a passionate and militant defender of universalism; struggling against the particular and sectarian distinctions that his contemporaries had associated with the Christ-event, he refuses to engage in obscurantist defenses of the faith; he believes in miracles and says he has experienced them, but he does not invoke them to demonstrate the truth: 'Christian discourse must, unwaveringly, refuse to be the discourse of miracle, so as to be the discourse of the conviction that bears a weakness within itself' (Badiou, 2003b, p. 51). Paul rejects all contingent categories in the discussion of the truth; thus too for him, 'the discourse of wisdom is definitively obsolete' (Badiou, 2003b, p. 58).

Modern Poetry and Truth-Process: The Case of Mallarmé

Badiou views the 20th century as a time of promise but not of delivery on the promise, a time of threshold but not the crossing of the threshold. When he makes these assertions he is referring to the century's frustrated goals of emancipation and rebirth, and the reality of its catastrophic wars and failed ideologies. As Badiou considers the variety of disciplinary purviews that have been invoked to explain this liminal century, he does not accede to the 'mistress of the moment: History' (Badiou, 2007, p. 1), which he sees as lacking philosophical depth and cogency. That is not to say that he is somehow indifferent to history; it is simply to deny the availability of the century's great truths to the prevailing schools of (Hegelian, Marxian, Crocean) historicism. Badiou prefers to focus on those creative works which originate in alienation and move toward emancipation, but also toward an encounter with emptiness: 'The century's militants, whether in politics, science, the arts or any other passion, think that man is realized not as a fulfillment, or as an outcome, but as absent to himself, torn away from what he is, and that it is this tearing away which is the basis of every adventurous greatness' (2007, p. 92). This citation comes from *The Century*, a book in which Badiou assigns poetry the leading symbolic role in deciphering the modern period: 'The Age of Poets' is said to begin with Hölderlin, who antedates the modern era, and is followed by Rimbaud, Mallarmé, Mandelstam, St.-Jean Perse, Breton, Brecht and Pessoa (Badiou, 1999, pp. 69–77). This period begins at a point when the relationship between philosophy, mathematics and the arts is muddled; 'philosophy is captive either of the sciences (positivisms) or of politics (Marxisms)', while the poem is still involved in 'philosophical poeticizing' (Badiou, 2003a, pp. 97, 100). Given this oppressive situation, those rare poets who succeed at liberating the poem do so because of their nomadic status: 'That nomadic wandering, as Perse says, should be the principle at the heart of man, even in its absence, is an apt geographic and wayfaring metaphor for an epoch proud of being *without security*' (Badiou, 2007, p. 92).

As a reader of poetry, Badiou respects the work's materiality and singularity as a work of art. Great poems are seen to comport a strong affective component (joy, love, fidelity, passion) that functions through the mind and senses in ways that are impossible to fully explicate. The poem is an inert object, without utilitarian value, but it serves as a paradigm for the problem of learning itself. This fact that art produces truths requires that one discard any purely aesthetic orientation in the poetry classroom, or any purely technical approach to pedagogy. Unfortunately in many sectors the teaching of poetry has continued under regimes that elude the truth-process by resorting to outdated (mimetic, aestheticist or identitarian) premises. These only serve to marginalize the poem's eternal moment or its instantiation of a truth process, depriving it of its mystery and emotional force. In contrast to these non-intrinsic views of the work, for Badiou the poem—like the artwork generally—is an irreplaceable and incommensurable vehicle of truth. Not only is his theory of truth-process fundamental to his analysis of poetry but it also constitutes the nucleus of a genuine philosophy of education.

'To arrange the forms of knowledge in such a way that some truth may come to pierce a hole in them', poetry (and art) needs to be free of the conceptual constraints of the past. Badiou's chapter on the relations between philosophy and poetry outlines three orientations that have predominated but are no longer adequate to our time: the Parmenidan, the Platonic and the Aristotelian. In the first, there is an effective fusion (or 'suture') between the subjective authority of the poem and the validity of statements held as philosophical. In the second, philosophy excludes the poem, maintaining its 'argumentative distance' since poetry is seen as a seduction, a fascination. In the third, philosophy categorizes the poem, including the knowledge of the poem within itself; thus the poem is reduced to the status of an aesthetic object (Badiou, 2003a, pp. 91–108). Badiou sees these three relations as inadequate to our day, and calls for a fourth relation in which the poem would not be a rival to philosophy but would be free 'as a singular operation of truth' (Badiou, 2003a, p. 98). The first crystallizing moment in this regard was found in Mallarmé, the poet who, as I argue below, clarified the operations and site of poetry as existing in 'pure presence': 'Only the poem accumulates the means of thinking outside-place, or beyond all place, "on some vacant and superior surface," what of the present does not let itself be reduced to its reality, but summons the eternity of its presence: "A Constellation, icy with forgetting and desuetude" ' (Badiou, 2003a, p. 99). Before turning to Mallarmé it will be necessary to examine Badiou's definition of truth-processes.

To follow Badiou, it is only by means of truth-process that a subject can pierce through the existing bodies of knowledge and beyond the constraints and motivations of pure self-interest; the subject itself does not exist prior to this irruptive event. Truth-processes occur in three different components: the 'event', which is immediate and transitory and cannot be reproduced or communicated; the 'fidelity' to that event, which endures over time, allowing the subject to resist the 'plenitude' of the current knowledge situation and to experience its effective emptiness; and the 'truth' itself, which amounts to the slow gathering of the results of one's investigation. Citing the process-thinking of Spinoza regarding human self-knowledge and self-interest, or what Spinoza calls 'perseverance in being', Badiou states that the pursuit of the truth lies *outside* the boundaries of such a natural situation and ordinary behavior: 'To belong to the situation is everyone's natural destiny, but to belong to the composition of a subject of truth concerns a particular route, a sustained break, and it's very difficult to know how this composition is to be superimposed upon or combined with the simple perseverance-of-self' (Badiou, 2002, p. 46). Unfortunately much of the current pedagogical orthodoxy requires that this *how* of truth-discovery be quantified and known ahead of time, predicated as the outcomes or goals of the academic experience. The emphasis on performance renders the learning subject less particular, less dynamic and more shielded against being impacted by the event. To prevent such preemptive institutional steps, educators must remain true to their own desire (here one sees the abiding impact on Badiou of the work of Lacan).

One can identify the elements of truth-process in Badiou's discussions of Mallarmé's *Coup de dés* (*A Cast of Dice*, 1897), an experimental work constituted by ten double-folio sheets including large amounts of white space and an accentuated, figural arrangement of heavily encoded and polysemic words—in diverse typefaces and sizes—arranged across the page. The poem is centered on the notion of chance and the indeterminate themes reflected at every compositional level (lexical, tropic, syntactic, graphic, semantic, figural). For Badiou the poem possesses a dramatic structure set within the space of pure possibility: 'Poetry is the stellar assumption of that pure undecidable, against a background of nothingness, that is an action which one can only *know* whether it has taken place inasmuch as one *bets* upon its truth' (2005b, p. 192). In terms of the 'event' of *A Cast of Dice*, its piercing through the forms of knowledge, that is provided by the 'shipwreck' (though the word *naufrage* is not mentioned) in whose wake the poem is gradually assembled. The 'fidelity' to that 'event' is based on the recognition of its undecidability, the confrontation with the void, the abyss, a point clarified by the images of dissipation and evanescence, such that the imminent prospect of shipwreck, or of death, is rendered inconsequential even as its certainty is confirmed and universalized. This is to enter into the space of pure possibility, or what scientific thinkers from Ilya Prigogine to Michel Serres refer to as 'stochastics' as the study of apparent randomness in the organization of complex structures. Mallarmé was experimenting with the principles of chance and the hypothesis that somehow, by a roll of the dice, chance could be abolished. The 'truth' of this process is developed as the poem evolves into a complex, multi-layered conclusion, a forcing of its new knowledge onto the stage of European modernity.

There is no reference in the poem to an external action; the only significant action is what happens within the poem, in the purely interior 'working through' of the subject's fidelity to the event. As Badiou writes, 'The non-being "there is," the pure and cancelled occurrence of the gesture, are precisely what thought proposes to render eternal' (2005b, pp. 191–2). If one can contemplate the absolute event that will abolish chance independently of that event existing, one's awareness can be raised to include a double configuration or coincidence of opposites (appearance/disappearance, being/non-being). This is the sense for Badiou of Mallarmé's reference to the concept of the number as such: 'the one Number which can be no other'. In the fictive narrative of *A Cast of Dice* the reader is led along an itinerary that is impossible to gloss here, but which Badiou has faithfully rendered, almost with the precision of a stylistic critic. In the following passage one sees the figure of the captain, the one piece of evidence on the basis of which the reader is to formulate the 'name' of the shipwreck, the chance 'event' that is alluded to throughout the poem: 'the captain of the shipwrecked vessel, the "master" whose arm is raised above the waves, whose fingers tighten around the two dice whose casting upon the surface of the sea is at stake' (Badiou, 2005a, p. 193):

> THE MASTER   beyond outworn calculations
>   where the manoeuvre with the age
>
> appeared
>   inferring   once he gripped the helm
>   from this conflagration at his feet
>   of the unanimous horizon
>
>   which   prepares   itself
>   is tossed and merges
>   with the fist that would grip it
>
>   as one threatens   destiny and the winds
>
>   the one Number which can be   no other   (Mallarmé, 1956, n.p.)

As the poem concludes, the question arises: shall we interpret this confrontation with non-being and nothingness nihilistically? Does the language of poetry collapse into sameness with the language of base commerce? Badiou's response is a decisive 'no' insofar as Mallarmé has arrived at 'an equivalence of gesture (casting the dice) and non-gesture (not casting the dice). ... That "nothing" has taken place therefore means solely that nothing *decidable within the situation* could figure the event as such. By causing the place of the poem to prevail over the idea that an event could be calculated therein, the poem realizes the essence of the event itself, which is precisely that of being, from this point of view, incalculable' (Badiou, 2005b, p. 197).

I draw on Renato Poggioli to further develop Badiou's understanding of Mallarmé. The Italian comparativist, born in 1907, possessed the same desire to evaluate the ontological weight of modern poetry and see within it the clues to the state of our civilization. There is a remarkable coincidence to be discovered in the two men's intense engagements with Mallarmé and Perse. To begin with, both thinkers focus on a brand of modern poetry that reaches back inclusively to the Romantic era; by embracing such a broad conception of modernity, they both avoid the inherent localisms and the emphasis on particular movements that has restricted our understanding of the roots of 20th century poetry. After the groundbreaking work of the romantics, one arrives at Symbolism, which continues the process Badiou refers to as the 'age of poets', which is also the era of Decadence, the term preferred by Poggioli in his exhilarating discussions of Baudelaire, Gautier, Mallarmé, Verlaine, Laforgue, Yeats, D'Annunzio and others. These discussions depict what is at heart a continuum from the early 19th century to the mid-20th century and thereby challenge any interpretation of literary Modernism as a self-enclosed period that broke with all that preceded it. Thus from the Symbolists or Decadents one passes almost seamlessly to the Crepuscular or Neo-Decadent poets such as Gozzano, Corazzini, Pound and Pessoa, who also saw civilization as declining and responded with a kind of modern mannerism, a syncretic style that combined components of diverse styles, including Neoclassicism and tendencies of the avant-garde. Poggioli's effective merger of the notion of decadence with that of modernity is supported by his demonstration of the widespread experience of alienation among the great modern poets. By stressing these poets' active continuation of the literary traditions of the past—even when their assumptions in this regard are 'unwritten'—he distinguishes their practice from the clinging to a passive tradition (the 'reactionary ideal') as well as from the 'alienation from tradition' that prevailed among many in the avant-garde. In essence, Poggioli is documenting what Badiou calls poetry's pursuit of its own laws, its own operational language and presence. Poggioli does this by reformulating historical criteria and periodizations that had gone unquestioned by the literary orthodoxy. His vision of the historian as, in Schlegel's term, a 'retrospective prophet' refers to a re-excavation of the past in which the pursuit of 'value' is elevated over the pursuit of 'interest' (Poggioli, 1965, p. 232). While interest only accounts for logical motivations, value accounts for irrational motivations including the sentiment and instinct. By calling Poggioli a retrospective prophet, I mean to refer to his ability to draw critical connections over great distances of time and space, and specifically his view of Romanticism and Decadentism as dynamic stages in the formation of the modern collective imagination. This paradigmatic approach is similar to Badiou's engagement of truth in the same periods. Positioned as an equal partner with mathematics and philosophy, poetry asserts itself as the missing link in the human self-awareness of late modernity. Thus, for Badiou and Poggioli alike, it is the modern poets who can best articulate the changed situation of being, language and truth that came about in the 20th century.

Both Poggioli and Badiou dedicate lengthy discussions to Mallarmé's *L'après-midi d'une faune* (*The Afternoon of a Faun*) and pay close attention to style, specifically the complex logical structure, syntax, and rhetorical stratification that Mallarmé presents in the poem's two alternating modes: the obliquely lyrical and descriptive passages and the narrative framework provided by the faun's internal monologue. Both thinkers assess the revolutionary nature of Mallarmé's poetics, his sense of the void and the emptying-out in the event, of the figure of the poet. Both thinkers are careful not to conflate the figures of the faun and the poet, a common error among critics; and both examine the lengthy and purifying evolution of the poem's composition in Mallarmé's life over a number of years. In his commentary on the poem's narrative of the faun's failed seduction of two nymphs, Poggioli shows that the work is not the poet's repetition of the faun's song. On the contrary, the setting is one of moral sublimation, in particular of that spiritual elevation achieved through art. This is not simple, as the poetry jealously veils its deeper meaning. The figure of the faun is seen, after the frustration of his erotic adventure at noonday, to retreat into memory as he seeks in his long afterthought to reconstruct in fantasy the moment of seduction, even at the risk of self-delusion. In exploring the 'contradictory law of the psyche' Poggioli highlights the insights of the poet into the problems of repression and the unconscious. In short, the poem is prophetic of a future form of expression—that of abstract art—even as it retains its relationship to the classical genre of the pastoral eclogue, and it ultimately represents the 'steady and gradual spiritualization of its essential erotic motive' (Poggioli, 1975, p. 310). In his discussion of *The Afternoon of a Faun*, Badiou writes: 'Mallarmé replaces the old romantic question of dream and reality with that of the evental origin of the true and of its relation to the givenness of a place. These are the components of the mystery' (Badiou, 2005b, p. 130).

Badiou and Poggioli share an unusual enthusiasm for the poetry of St.-Jean Perse, especially the epic *Anabasis*, and that of Paul Claudel. While Poggioli's considerations of these poets' novelty is phrased in more literary terms, he would definitely share the Badiouian idea of poets moving along the 'diagonal' with respect to the dominant ideologies of the century; herein lies their great worth in orienting students towards truth. As David Harvey writes, Poggioli is a critic who aims towards becoming, and not towards being, as the Classicalist and postmodernist attitudes would have it. Harvey is highly skeptical of the Heideggerian emphasis on being which has been a key component of much postmodernist theory (Harvey, 1989, p. 359). Here too there is a syntony with Badiou's ideas on the subject. Badiou is a proponent of a 'radical multiplicity' that is not constrained or 'ensnared' in Heidegger's 'onto-theology' and 'destinal apparatus' of the 'one'. In response to Heidegger's declaration that 'a darkening of the world comes about on Earth', a darkening that will be accompanied by 'the flight of the gods, the destruction of the Earth, the vulgarization of man, the preponderance of the mediocre', Badiou writes:

> Countering Heidegger, we should declare: the illumination of the world has always accompanied its immemorial darkening. Thus the flight of the gods is also the beneficial event of men's taking-leave of them; the destruction of the Earth is also the conversion that renders it amenable to active thinking; the vulgarization of man is also the egalitarian irruption of the masses onto the stage of history; and the preponderance of the mediocre is also the dense lustre of what Mallarmé called 'restrained action'. (Badiou, 2004, p. 40, citing Heidegger, 1980, p. 38)

In order to exemplify the opening onto the multiple, Badiou also cites Lucretius, the poet of nature's constant changes and human evolution, who engages the poem 'to confront thinking directly with that subtraction from the one constituted by inconsistent infinity' (Badiou, 2004, p. 41). As the singer of the kaleidoscopic evanescence of the natural world, Lucretius reminds us of Badiou's commitment to truth and its connections to science and the matheme.

Conclusion

To inquire into the impact of Badiou's work on the field of education is to recognize, first of all, the great value placed on the pursuit of truth throughout his opus, from *Being and Event* to the topical works in which the philosophy of the event is applied to questions of history, poetry, the arts and politics, and mathematics and science. Badiou's philosophical expertise is complemented by an expertise in mathematics and set-theory. *Being and Event* thus possesses the purity, solidity and stature of an epochal work. Since Badiou possesses great fluency with the most important scientific discoveries of our age, the educational impact of reading him is direct and firsthand. By the same token, one finds an abundance of ancillary material that invites poets, scientists, musicians and mathematicians, into the pedagogical discussion. This makes the books divulgative and educational in a way comparable to those of Whitehead, who formulated a philosophy of actual occasions, comparable in many respects to Badiou's philosophy of the event, and also wrote books on intellectual history that interconnected movements in the arts and sciences. As Whitehead once wrote:

> Every age manages to find modes of classification which seem fundamental starting points for the researches of the special sciences. Each succeeding age discovers that the primary classifications of its predecessors will not work. In this way a doubt is thrown upon all formulations of laws of Nature which assume these classifications as firm starting points. A problem arises. Philosophy is the search for its solution. (Whitehead, 1968, p. 2)

This sense of philosophy's role in updating the modes of classification is consonant with Badiou's implicit pedagogy. As he writes, 'Let us recall that the only education is an education *by* truths. The entire, insistent problem is that there be truths, without which the philosophical category of truth is entirely empty and the philosophical act nothing but an academic quibble' (2005b, pp. 14–15).

Notes

1. See Said, 2004, p. 13: 'It is worth insisting ... that attacking the abuses of something is not the same thing as dismissing or entirely destroying that thing. So, in my opinion, it has been the abuse of humanism that discredits some of humanism's practitioners without discrediting humanism itself.'
2. See Nussbaum, 1997, p. 295: 'We do not fully respect the humanity of our fellow citizens— or cultivate our own—if we do not wish to learn about them, to understand their history, to appreciate the differences between their lives and ours. We must therefore construct a liberal education that is not only Socratic, emphasizing critical thought and respectful argument, but also pluralistic, imparting an understanding of the histories and contributions of groups with whom we interact, both within our nation and in the increasingly international sphere of business and politics. If we cannot teach our students everything they will need to know to be good citizens, we may at least teach them what they do not know and how they may inquire ... . Above all, we can teach them how to argue, rigorously and critically, so that they can call their minds their own.'

References

Badiou, A. (1999) *Manifesto for Philosophy*. Followed by two essays: 'The (Re)turn of philosophy *itself*' and 'Definition of philosophy', N. Madarasz, trans., ed. and intro. (Albany, State University of New York Press).

Badiou, A. (2002) *Ethics: An essay on the understanding of evil*, P. Hallward, trans. and intro. (London, New York, Verso).

Badiou, A. (2003a) *Infinite Thought: Truth and the return to philosophy*, O. Feltham & J. Clemens, trans. and ed. (New York, Continuum).

Badiou, A. (2003b) *Saint Paul: The foundation of universalism*, R. Brassier, trans. (Stanford, CA, Stanford University Press).

Badiou, A. (2004) *Theoretical Writings*, R. Brassier & A. Toscano, ed. and trans. (London and New York, Continuum).

Badiou, A. (2005a) *Being and Event*. O. Feltham, trans. (London and New York, Continuum).

Badiou, A. (2005b) *Handbook of Inaesthetics*, A. Toscano, trans. (Stanford, CA, Stanford University Press).

Badiou, A. (2007) *The Century*, A. Toscano, trans. (Cambridge, Polity Press).

Barthes, R. (2005) *The Neutral. Lecture course at the College de France (1977–1978)*, R. E. Krauss & D. Hollier, trans. Text established, annotated, and presented by T. Clerc under the direction of E. Marty (New York, Columbia University Press).

Harvey, D. (1989) *The Condition of Postmodernity: An enquiry into the origins of cultural change* (Oxford, Basil Blackwell).

Heidegger, M. (1980) *Introduction to Metaphysics*, R. Mannheim, trans. (New Haven, CT, Yale University Press).

Mallarmé, S. (1956) *Un coup de des jamais n'abolira le hazard*, D. Aldan, English trans. (New York, Tiber Press).

Nussbaum, M. (1997) *Cultivating Humanity. A classical defense of reform in liberal education* (Cambridge, MA, Harvard University Press).

Nussbaum, M. (2001) *Upheavals of Thought: the Intelligence of Emotions* (New York, Cambridge University Press).

Poggioli, R. (1965) *The Spirit of the Letter* (Cambridge, MA, Harvard University Press).

Poggioli, R. (1975) *The Oaten Flute* (Cambridge, MA, Harvard University Press).

Readings, B. (1996) *The University in Ruins* (Cambridge, MA, Harvard University Press).

Said, E. (2000) *Reflections on Exile and Other Essays* (Cambridge, MA, Harvard University Press).

Said, E. (2004) *Humanism and Democratic Criticism* (New York, Columbia University Press).

Slaughter, S. & Rhoades, G. (2004) *Academic Capitalism and the New Economy: Markets, state, and higher education* (Baltimore, MD, Johns Hopkins University Press).

Whitehead, A. N. (1968) *Nature and Life* (New York, Greenwood Press).

Wilden, A. (1987) *The Rules are No Game. The Strategy of Communication* (London, Routledge & Kegan Paul).

3

Badiou's Challenge to Art and its Education: Or, 'art cannot be *taught*—it can however *educate*!'

JAN JAGODZINSKI

.... the only education is an education by truths (IN, p. 14)

Badiou's writings on contemporary art and aesthetics present perhaps an impossible challenge to art and its education in the way they are presently hegemonically envisioned and taught within art and design schools, as well as secondary schools. This chapter attempts to provide the framework of Badiou's assessment of contemporary art and his stance towards aesthetics, which he specifically terms 'inaesthetics' to differentiate his position from the way philosophy has traditionally taken art as its object. As Badiou recognizes Lacan as a significant influence on his work, I will also draw on Lacanian concepts in my argument. Indeed, Badiou understands his work as following a deviant and alternative contemporary philosophy whose origin, contra Kant, is not based in the conceptual but in the Lacanian Real, which includes Nietzsche and his followers. I end by assessing his position to the teaching of art in general by maintaining my own aphorism: 'Art cannot be *taught*—it can, however, *educate*!' as a response to Badiou's demand that—when it comes to contemporary art—'something else is possible' (Theses, p. 110) and it is imperative 'to speak the unspeakable' (SA).

The Subject of Art

Badiou has given us a number of significant presentations[1] that provide his assessment of contemporary art to answer his critics as to his silence concerning their various media-ted forms after cinema, the later of which he has very little to say except that it is an 'impure' art form. Critics have rightfully taken him to task on this (Ling, 2006). I will start with the later essay first, 'The Subject of Art' (SA), translating its premises into 'Lacanese' since this is where the artistic event is most clearly elaborated. Badiou begins his presentation on art by offering three levels of signification of being. The three levels, as I read them, follow Lacan's three psychic registers. The first level, being *qua* being, designates *pure multiplicity*, and refers to the Lacanian Symbolic register of language, law and its obscene supplement of illegality, often referred to as the big Other, *theorized mathematically by Badiou as an open system*. His second level refers to existence—to something that 'is'. This would be Lacan's Imaginary register in the way that pure multiplicity becomes 'framed'. Hence, this is a categorization, an *inclusion* or sub-set that belongs to the broad set of elements that compose the first level of being as the symbolic order, which Badiou describes as 'the encyclopedia. This is 'the general system of predicative knowledge internal to a situation: i.e., what everyone knows about politics, sexual difference, culture, art, technology, etc'. (TW, p. 146).

The relationship between pure multiplicity of being (symbolic order or big Other) and existence of that multiplicity (the psychic Imaginary) in the here and now has been overwhelmingly theorized through various forms of constructivism—hermeneutics, phenomenology, Freudian psychoanalysis, structuralism, and post-structuralism—wherein the transcendental logic of the Law (the metastructure or 'state') that organizes the legal and illegal combinations of the parts that make up the symbolic whole is always, at the same time, managing the excess parts (the many possible imaginary sub-sets or parts) as to whether they do or do not belong to the larger whole. 'It is the bond, this proximity that language builds between presentation (membership/elements) and representation (parts/inclusion), which ground the conviction that the state does not exceed the situation by too much, or that it remains commensurable' (BE, p. 288). To open up this system, Badiou introduces the 'truth' of an event or happening from the void of the Lacanian Real, a true act of creation that is capable of 'subtracting' itself from the existing transcendental logic. This is thought itself, or put another way 'thought thinking itself' that takes seriously the question as to 'what is possible' in relation to what 'is' to produce the *unthought* as that which is not—the proper site of an event. In this materialist dialectic the question of the event is *thought solely by art*.

In *Being and Event*, these three registers are theorized mathematically through three developments in set theory. The ontology of thinking pure multiplicity (the Law of the big Other) is covered by the set theory of Cantor; the logic of thinking appearance as being-in-a-world (the psychic Imaginary of existence) is covered by Grothendieck's category theory, and finally, the subject-ive thinking of truth, of thought itself, is supported by Cohen's concepts of genericity and forcing so as to grasp how a Real event unfolds for the subject in the aspiration of truth and then in the capacity to produce statements (the forcing operation) from the local status of truth that is being pursued. Badiou, therefore, mobilizes the 'state of the art' of complexity theory to theorize Being as an open system.

The happening of the event is a 'subtractive' process as opposed to the 'purifying' process of mathematics. Mathematics is unable to inform the event. They are separate spheres as indicated by the gap of the ampersand—being & event. Badiou explains this subtractive procedure by first recognizing that the creative event is a negation; it *must* be a negation since it is an exception that stands apart from the current state of the 'situation'. Badiou however insists that although the creative event implies a negativity it must paradoxically affirm its identity apart from the *destructive* side of negation. Subtraction from the existing system is 'affirmative negation', and hence does not destroy the system but becomes *indifferent* to its laws. Subtraction exists apart from the negative part of negation—apart from destruction. Badiou is simply describing a truth of a new set of conditions that identify another set of phenomena that exist in the void of the system, in the Real, where they could not be named, but remained indeterminate, not recognized, in excess of the system when it comes to inclusion. In this sense, Badiou offers us a new nomadic politics, a dis-placed politics that has *no place*, characterized by 'an absolute equality' (Drawing, p. 48). This also characterizes his demand for art, to which I shall return.

Badiou, in a sense, posits multiple worlds. Einsteinian physics, as an event does not 'destroy' the Newtonian universe. Newtonian physics can still get a 'man' on the moon, but Einstein's relativity laws already define another universe, another world with different transcendental conditions suggesting other difficulties such as the relativity of time. Badiou uses his favorite example of Schoenberg's invention of atonality that is subtracted from three centuries of Western tonal music to present a truth event that becomes indifferent to the differences that compose the transcendental regime governing classical music. Classical music, however, does not stop. The event, therefore, happens not *in* this world (symbolic order) as it currently exists, rather it happens *for* this world, as a process *with and through it*, enriching it by punching a hole in current knowledge, presenting us with a truth; while a subject, for Badiou, is precisely the relationship between such an event and the world that the event affirmatively negates as an entirely new commitment emerges.

Badiou identifies the event as always being local, arising from a situation that is constructively understood. The event is always singular and *unheimlich*, leaving a *trace* in the world as it 'disappears'. Badiou defines this trace as 'what subsists in the world when the event disappears' (SA). The body of the new subjectivity is positioned between the trace of the event and the constructed world. This new emerging subject or new body belongs neither completely to the event (which has disappeared) and neither completely to the world (which remains in its constructed state). Properly speaking, this is a *new* subject—not a single personality but a *collective subject* that works out the new paradigm, belonging partially to the event through fidelity to the trace and partially to the world by what it affirmatively and 'forcibly' adds to it. Developing the event acquires a certain style or 'stylus' in Berel Lang's (1982) sense, in the way it 'cuts' out a new domain by establishing a 'body' of work, what Badiou calls a 'configuration' (IN, p. 12). Style emerges in spite of the artist's conscious intentions; it is a surplus, which cannot be totally controlled, but a by-product—a singular mode and therefore unconscious, revealing unconscious sub-graphemes, the place of 'formless form' or 'inform'. This then becomes the artistic body composed of a particular sensibility. Such is a creative act 'seemingly' *ex nihilo*—emerging as a truth event from the void of the Real (see Badiou, 2003). When it comes to the truth event, art is therefore given a priority status compared to the other domains of truth generation: science, politics, and love that he favors (as opposed to economics or theology, for instance).

Badiou maintains that the two warring subjective paradigms, each the inverse of the other, characterize the contemporary situation. On one side we have a collapse between the subject and the body, with the body attempting to become victorious. The subject is reduced to the body, or *immanently* 'is' the body. Badiou identifies this as the body of the drives (*Triebe*), characterized by the excesses of *jouissance* as theorized most vehemently by Slavoj Žižek throughout his entire *oeuvre*, exploring its limits as a concrete unity. This is an experimentation of 'death in life', and we can characterize this as a sublime aesthetic of ugliness where total body tattooing and piercing would be exemplary, as would the 'high performance' body art of Stelarc, Orlan or Chris Burden. But, the issue between subject and body is not so easily resolved. Badiou also makes a distinction between those artists whose performances are 'without the body', where the body has been idealized and those 'within the body' (Theses, p. 119), like dancers and actors in the cinema. In some high performance art it is difficult to tell which is which.[2] Hal Foster (1996) has characterized such art as the 'return of the [Lacanian] Real', trying to sort out its different responses. Perhaps the most extreme case is the Chinese performance artist, Zhu Yu who reportedly ate a human fetus claiming that, when it comes to cannibalism, he was questioning the space between morality and the law. While Deleuze is perceived by Badiou as his foil against difference and multiplicity, this body of *jouissance* is best explained by Deleuze and Guattari concept of the body-without-organs (BwO), which is comparable to Lacan's 'body in pieces' of the pre-subjective self. In its most radical form, this body *is* the subject, and when it comes to advocating the emergence of a new truth for art, my position has always been to do away with any forms of transcendentalism, including Lacan's emphasis on the Phallus (jagodzinski, 2006a).

On the other side of the ledger is the body of sacrifice where the subject is completely *separated* from the body. Badiou calls this an idealist paradigm—a theological and metaphysical philosophy of the subject. This can be characterized as the modernist technological dream whereby 'mind' can be eventually down-loaded into a functioning computer (as in the theory of Hans Moravec), like in the movie *Johnny Mnemonic*. The body has been 'sacrificed' to technology in a cyborgian scenario of total control, raising in Lacan's terms, the obsessive discursive question, 'Am I alive or dead?' that plagues science fiction narrative like *Bladerunner* and *Battlestar Galactica* where the line between human and machine cannot be demarcated. This is but one side of the fantasy; the other fantasy is a transcendentalism whereby mind as spirit participates in another world, a hereafter that is not *of* the world. This is no longer 'death in life' but a transformation into its very opposite—a 'life in death' since the promise of discarding the body through sacrifice offers an other worldly freedom. Terrorism, as in suicide bombers, present the extreme case, since their sacrifice for the Cause is made to gain pleasure beyond suffering as a promise of a transcendent world. In contrast to the sublime aesthetic, we have sublime Beauty that does not participate *in* the world.

The body event in the first paradigm is caught being *inside the world*—a raw Materialism that reaches its limit in death, while the second paradigm of the Mind is caught *outside of the world*, as an Idealism that celebrates *Geist* as Man or Man as *Geist* to reach the limit of death. So, the first position is always *full*, life is paradoxically satisfied by the *jouissance* of the drives. Art is characterized here by an 'in your face' Realism—as *matter* that is 'in' the world, as the *unformed* that is actively sought. The second position is characterized by *lack*, the fulfillment of which is found in transcendence, in a Utopian form that is contemplatively sought. Satisfaction is found in sacrifice as deferment in anticipation of what is to come. Hence this subjectivity is characterized by 'transcendent difference'. Experimentation takes places in the transcendent world and not in the world proper. It is not empirically pragmatic.

What is common to both positions is therefore the intensity of death; although death is precisely interpreted differently, both positions arrive at the same limit destination. We can say that in the art of the body Real, death is *in* the world, whereas in the ideal spirit of mind, art is a projected utopian ideal *out* of this world. The binaries are held together as atheistic/theistic, dystopian/utopian where production always aims at the limit. They are hyper-spectacular in this sense, characterized by 'too near' disgust of sublime Abject (like the *Saw* horror series, the pun should be obvious) and unattainable 'too far' of sublime Beauty respectively (think of the film *SimOne*). Badiou maintains that this war between *jouissance* and sacrifice where the power of death is arrived at through extremes does not provide an opening for artistic creation. A third paradigm or 'possibility' is needed that is outside the power of death.

What then is this third possibility? Badiou names it 'immanent difference' which begins to sound like Deleuze's 'transcendent empiricism' in the way he goes about describing it. Badiou describes the in-between space of these two extremes as being engaged in the world (in 'life') so as to create affirmatively something *for* it. Here the new body that has a fidelity to the trace is constructed through 'subtraction' as mentioned earlier. It is a process of creative production not reducible to the *identification* via the body where the trace of the event *is* the body itself; or *separated* as mind where the trace has been lost to the world, for the subject has identified with this trace via the mind in the absoluteness of the event, as in a god-like longing for its full realization. One wonders what particular theological propositions, in Badiou's terms, are therefore 'empty' of truth? Badiou believes that contemporary art is in search of such a body that is not caught by *jouissance* and sacrifice, where the artist is therefore *for* the world; that is engaged in it by maintaining 'the distinction between the body on one side and the trace of the event on the other side' (SA).

Badiou's Five Problems

Five problems present themselves for such a potential possibility, which Badiou briefly outlines but does not fully discuss. They lead up to his articulation of the artistic event as a form of subtraction. The first problem is a question of the subjective *distance* from the event, which must avoid the complete disappearance of an event's trace as a collapse back into the body, or the transcendence of the trace into some absolutist outer worldly principle—exemplified best, I believe, by post-Romantic New Age art movements, especially ecological idealizations where

Nature is imbued with Gaia spirituality. The event must necessarily remain affirmative despite its negation, which forms a rupture, a cut or break with the laws that govern the present situation. The second problem is a question of the very nature of the trace since, as an affirmation of the event it has to remain *in* the world, whereas the event is not exactly in it, forming the initial burst, and then vanishing. The third problem is how the new subject-ive body is constituted in relation to the trace of the event? The fourth problem refers to the practical consequences of the materialist creation of the new? Then finally, Badiou refers to the problem of 'immanent infinity', which speaks to a potentiality—alluding to the Deleuzian virtuality of infinite consequences. However, virtuality plays no part in Badiou's thinking, which, as I argue at the end of this chapter when it comes to the *doing* of art—of art-ing, is a weakness. Immanent infinity avoids the experimentation of the limits that define the current aporia of contemporary art where death is the limit by recognizing the many *actualizations* of the artistic work that are affirmations *for* the world—as 'life' itself, which again leads to a DeleuzeGuattarian problematic.

Perhaps a primary example of all five problems is an installation performance done by the Chilean-born New York artist Alfred Jaar who was commissioned in 2000 (I assume as a millennium project) by the city council of Skoghall, Sweden, to build a cultural place of community gathering since the city did not have one. Skoghall was the site of the world's largest paper mill. It was a company town shaped by industrial paternalism but bereft of culture. Jaar proceeded to build the *Skoghall Konsthall* entirely out of the paper made by the mill and then preceded to have an exhibition of young Swedish artists, inviting the press and the government to the opening. Twenty-four hours after the festive opening, and according to Jaar's plan, the building was ignited and allowed to burn down and collapse in on itself, despite the protests and pleas to salvage the wood (Jaar's background as an architect made this a possibility). The immolation of the building highlighted the community's impoverished cultural life through Jaar's spectacular orchestration of heightened expectations brought on by the exhibition; and then his withdrawal and destruction of the community's desire by his act staged a trauma of loss and shock. Jaar's claim was that the community could not invite an outsider artist simply to produce a sense of 'art' and 'community' in a site where they weren't supported in the first place. It was now up to the city council along with the paper mill company to form their own cultural initiative.

Jaar's installation performance certainly took aim at the void of Skoghall's Real: the unwillingness, silence and the lack of political initiative to generate a cultural center. Jaar has staged an artistic event that is *for* the world; despite its negativity (destruction) it remains an affirmation as a trace that must be followed by the community of Skoghall if a new body is to emerge at this site. However, it also raises questions within Badiou's own proposals. One could say that Jaar's installation performance 'inscribes the inexistent' as Badiou (Drawing, 46) insists, and it practices a new sort of politics, as 'an action without place', 'an international and nomadic creation with—as in a work of art—a mixture of violence, abstraction and final peace' (Drawing, 48). On the other hand, the disappearance of the work that strengthens it as a form of witnessing takes it in the direction of theatre, especially *theatre exemplified by the cinema* as an art of *loss*. For Badiou, cinema is an impure art because of its 'passing:' 'Cinema is an art of the perpetual past, in the sense that it institutes the past of the pass [*la passe*]' (IN, 78). Such an art of loss 'is not of subtraction but *purification*, and hence of destruction (or again, an art not of the void nor the voided, but rather of *voiding*' (Ling, 2006, p. 272, author's emphasis). There is no *remainder*, or rather the remainder can only be sustained by Jaar's rehearsing this event as a simulacra during talks or critics remarking on its effects. Consequently, as Ling argues, Badiou's inaesthetic conceptions are 'symptomatic of his mathematical leanings: if art thinks the event (at the precise point at which mathematics itself falters) it does so by virtue of its relation—or rather, non-relation—to the matheme' (p. 271). *The artistic work is therefore inseparable from its mathematization as it asymptotically strives for purification despite its initial subtraction.* We can use Jaar to point to an inverted problematic—the recuperation of loss as destruction rather than the destruction as loss.

British artist Mark Wallinger's (Bois *et al.*, 2008) eight-month installation called *State Britain* took place from January 15 to August 27, 2007 at the Tate Britain, London. This was a faithful restoration, *in every detail*, of Brian Haw's Parliament Square protest against the economic sanctions against Iraq by the coalition of the willing. On May 23, 2006 an Act of Parliament was passed that prohibited unauthorized demonstrations within a one-kilometer radius of Parliament Square. Haw's protest was promptly removed, but not before Wallinger had documented the work, enabling him to reconstruct the protest by placing it *exactly* just over the one-kilometer line that also ran through the Tate Britain.[3] Wallinger's installation, placed at the '*edge* of the situation's void' as Badiou insists (BF, 113), resurrected the 'loss' as an *affirmation*. Within British parliamentary law such protests do not *count*; that is, Haw's action is an exclusionary element that has no place in the democratic system as it is currently defined, existing in the void. It is now made to re-*appear* as an event, a subject-point of a 'new realism' (BF, 118) as Badiou would want it.

Badiou's articulates the 'world of art' as a relational process the artist undertakes between the chaos of sensibility,[4] articulated often as 'inform' or 'formless',[5] and form itself. An 'artistic event', for Badiou is 'a change in the formula of the world'. It's the emergence of form from the inform as a new *affirmative* disposition. Simply put, it is the relation of three terms: S (the chaos of sensibility as the inform), F (form) and F_1 (new disposition) of the formalization. In Alfredo Jaar's work, the question emerges, when is this new affirmative disposition created? The building of the *Skoghall Konsthall* has not yet created a new sensibility. It is the very intensity of burning it down that creates the rupture of the event, shaking the laws of the 'situation' or state of the affairs. In Wallinger's case, the 'resurrection' of what has been erased intervenes in the situation. We have a complication in Badiou's general formula of an artistic event where F is destroyed/resurrected, made absent/present so that F_1's *potentially* (as virtuality in Deleuzian sense) might be actualized. There is no guarantee that the trace of the event will be taken up by city council, the paper mill company or other member of the community; nor will the parliamentary act be overturned. The affirmative dimension of the artistic creation, in Jaar's case, *is a return to inform*, back to chaotic sensibility, whereas with Wallinger it is a return to form. Both return with a *difference*, as *Weiderkehr*.[6] The consequences of the immolation are left as a question mark as to whether its ethical plea in the void of the Real is to be answered since Jaar has staged a 'truth' concerning the situation. Ditto for Wallinger. The trace of an artistic event, as Badiou says, is like a 'manifesto', something 'like a new declaration'.

Jaar's installation-performance thus forms a new body in the artistic field in the way he explores the space between the private and the public in an epigrammatic and ephemeral way, where form and inform are in continual process of canceling each other out in an interval of time that sets of the event, the traces of which make declarations, but never offer actualizations. These are left to the witnesses of the event, affected by it so as to have fidelity with and to it *for* the world. The erasure of an object as an event, or its 'resurrection', *forces* a new viewing and a potential actualization as a result of the ethical demand it makes on witnesses of the event. The event emerges from the void of the Real where the truth of the artistic event—not in the Heideggerian sense of being hidden and secretive so that it can be revealed and released—is *created* and then exposed by the singularity of the contingent event. Another fine example would be the *disappearing* monument against Fascism in Hamburg constructed by Jochen (with Esther Shalev-Gerz). The lead surface of the column, covered in graffiti (including gunshot 'wounds'), slowly sank into the ground over a period from October 10, 1986 to November 10, 1993; its 'disappearance' addressing the void of the previous silence over fascism, which the graffiti (70,000 signatures) brought out. Jochen Gerz seems to confirm Badiou when he says 'the monument takes no sides. It is completely *indifferent*, so much so that one can't even get emotional'. As a new form it becomes indifferent to the previous rules of what a monument 'is'.

Jaar and Gertz produce a void or lack in being, rather than merely announcing presence, which Wallinger necessarily does (resurrect presence) to achieve the same aim. The staging of such artistic events answer Badiou's final concern of 'immanent infinity' and his plea that artistic responsibility during our contemporary obscure political times requires artistic experimentation that can develop a third subjective paradigm. Jaar, Gertz, Wallinger among others illustrate such a line of flight. This growing artistic body of work as subject-points in the process of truth show how a new form offers a 'direct relation' with the 'chaos of sensibility' thereby, presenting a 'new manner of thinking of the infinite itself' by accessing the 'infinity of the world as such' (quotes as culled from SA).

Badiou's Inaesthetic

Badiou's presentations on art have the underlying tow of his inaesthetics, which has proven to be a difficult concept to grasp since it attempts to leave philosophy's grasp of aesthetics behind; or rather, it attempts to make philosophy let go of its grasp of art so as to reposition its relationship to it.[7] The attempt can best be described utilizing Lacan's four discourses as they appear in Seminar XVII, *L'envers de la psychanalyse* (Lacan, 2006).[8] Art, as stated in the opening pages of Badiou's primary essay 'Art and Philosophy', written in 1997 as the lead essay that opens his *Handbook of Inaesthetics* (2005b), is characterized as the 'discourse of the hysteric' in relation to philosophy, which is its Master. The Master, however, always fails to provide the truth for the hysteric. She continually remains unsatisfied with his answers. He continually tries to please her, yet in the end the hysteric takes charge, ' "barring" him from mastery and becoming his mistress' (IN, p. 1), but on her terms. The truth of art, therefore, remains with her, for she cannot be *attained*.

Badiou's sex/gendering is purposeful here. The choice of designating art to be hysterical speaks to its refusal—ever since the 19ᵗʰ century when German Idealism (Baumgarten, Kant, Schelling, Schiller, Hegel) invented aesthetics and art as an autonomous sphere from which to transform the social order as desired by an aspiring class of *haute bourgeoisie*—to accept the truth that is being offered either by the discourse of the Master and more recently the discourse of the University, what Badiou calls the art of Empire or Imperial art (of designer capitalism). German Idealism steeped in Romanticism sets up a division between art and non-art, or art and everyday life, thus ushering in modernism. Art, in this context 'reveals' the workings of everyday life. It holds its secret and is encrypted within it. The pious philosopher as a silent witness, spellbound by the work, releases its secret—pre-Socratic truth as *aletheia*. In this regard, Heidegger stands as the quintessential Romantic.

Aesthetics in this view has taken art as its object either through the discourse of the Master or the University.[9] The Master discourse has always reduced art to a dogmatic, didactic and even therapeutic stance to 'cure' the hysteric, while the discourse of the University presents it as revelation that is specific to art through hermeneutical interpretation. In all cases art is *ethically* put to use.[10] Badiou wishes to change this. Succinctly stated on the inside cover of his 'handbook', 'inaesthetics' is 'a relation of philosophy to art that, maintaining that art itself is a producer of *truths*, makes no claim to turn art into an object for philosophy. Against aesthetic speculation, inaesthetics describes the strictly *intraphilosophical* effects produced by the independent existence of *some* works of art' (added emphasis) (IN, inside cover). The three words that I have emphasized (truth, intraphilosophical, and some) hold the key to grasping what Badiou is up to.

Inaesthetics as the new relationship to philosophy is a shift to the 'discourse of the Analyst' in Lacan's terms. Badiou concedes that art *produces* a truth, and that truth is found in the void of the Real (*objet a*). The philosopher must attempt to articulate rather than interpret its truth or to categorize it, adjudicate it through external norms of beauty, the abject, or taste and so on, or tell the truth about it if such truth lays *outside* its boundary. The relation of art to truth is therefore *singular* and *immanent* to the art's *effects* (IN, p. 9). This is a 'descriptive' relationship, describing the 'effects' of specific truth processes that are immanent and specific to particular (*some*) art. These are particular and identifiable artistic configurations. The description attempts to find both key (S_1) and secondary signifiers (S_2) that support or revolve around the void of the truth. Let me provide an example, one that the reader can easily imagine since copyright laws are always difficult to get around. While Badiou continually leans to poetry,[11] I intend to keep to the visual.

Tibor Kalman was the editor of *Colors*, the notorious magazine supported by Benetton, which enabled him to co-opt the corporation in his own way. I take this to be a contemporary *schizophrenic* position of addressing the void. He tricked them into doing responsible things in his own way. I also take his work as an example of what I call *indesign*; that is, corporate and consumer images that are folded in-and-on-themselves to produce a truth-effect. There are two digitally manipulated portraits I would like to 'analyze' in an inaesthetic way as a 'field of operations', one of them can be easily found through Google's image search—it is a standard portrait of Queen Elizabeth II dressed in royal regalia (i.e. tiara, sash, gloves) as can be found on the back of any paper currency in Britain. The difference is that she is *black*. Her lips have been exaggerated, blown up and her complexion changed just enough to give her a visible racial profile. The second picture is a portrait of Arnold Schwarzenegger from the chest up. His hair has become curly and his skin color closer to brown. He is smiling. As simple as these two examples are, they immediately denote a 'truth' through their effects as to the racial and ethnic mix of England and California respectively, which they govern and symbolically represent. The absent color white is the master signifiers (S_1), while black and brown respectively are the racially and ethnically secondary charged signifiers (S_2) that S_1 'represents'. The 'truth' of their representation is exposed as the void in the Real that supports both their politics and authority. Such an inaesthetic relationship is a 'rarefaction' of a *local* rather than a *general* situation, producing a *Wiederkehr* experience (a repetition that introduces difference) so that we must 'look' again—or 'think again' as Badiou would want it. *It forces us to think.* This operation is 'intraphilosophical' in the sense of the logic of a 'disjunctive synthesis' (Deleuze's term), whereby a compossibility (Leibnitz's term) is maintained between art and philosophy, neither one collapses into the other in any sort of dialectical move. It is therefore an affirmative practice 'producing' the truth of the Real. And, only *some* works of art do this.[12]

Badiou Exposed

There is a rivalry between Badiou and Deleuze as well as Rancière as to their respective aesthetic positions. Rancière[13] seems to wage war on both Badiou and Deleuze. Their differences, however, are helpful to expose Badiou's position, but I can only do this in a cursory manner given the space available here. Deleuze and Badiou form the greatest contrast given that the former emphasizes the dimension of sensation—of *aesthetics*; that is, perception and affects as they play themselves out on the BwO as a 'logic of sense' (Deleuze, 1990). Hence, from Deleuze and Guattari's perspective there is less of an argument concerning body art, regardless of whether it is 'with' or 'without' the body.[14] Badiou lies on the polar extreme. His notion of 'purification' leads to artistic truth as Idea, which for him becomes 'thinking'. Badiou is therefore a supporter of Conceptualism, which finds very little room in Deleuze's aesthetic. The visual artists he chooses (Malevich and Lombardi) are conceptual artists where virtually all aestheticism has been stripped away. Purification of an event by an artistic body of work is towards a distillation of the 'matheme' that underlies the artistic truth sought; this is more of an intellectual enterprise—like his ontological based mathematics. Hence, Badiou is often ineffectual dealing with arts that are 'impure' like cinema, and he has trouble with dance where the body's movement does not lend itself to easy purification or subtraction. Once this is understood, many things fall into place.

Let me illustrate Badiou's inaesthetic proposition by recalling a very funny scene from one of my favorite movies *Ghost World*, based on Daniel Cloves comic book series of the same name. The scene takes place in Roberta's summer art class 'for remedial students and fuck-ups'. During a critique, Roberta makes comments on a number of artworks and then finally comes to Margaret's sculpture, which is a jumble of wire hangers, seemingly haphazardly put together. Roberta asks Margaret to 'talk to us about it', to which Margaret replies with a pithy rhetorical response that it is her passionate statement about the *issue* of a woman's right to choose. Roberta is delighted and tells the class that this is an example of the 'higher category of art' she was speaking about that addresses 'emotion, politics, and spirituality'. Margaret's sculpture and her response cover all the basis of Badiou's inaesthetics. The sculpture does away with skill, it is stripped of aestheticism and so it cannot be commodified, thereby doing away with the seductions of 'presence' (like Mallarmé's poetry). Above all the truth of the work initiates thinking as Idea. The idea is essential, the minimalist sculpture is neither a description nor a sensual expression. It stands on its own, stripped bare, as it were, in its purity. Margaret's inaesthetic response is that of the analyst, referring to the event as the void of the horror of illegal abortions where women demonstrating for pro-choice wore tiaras made of wire hangers as signs of the backstreet and home abortions by desperate women who had no other place to turn. Her sculpture could be a 'subject point', one of many works in a 'sequence of artistic configuration' that would 'speak' to the truth of the trauma surrounding illegal abortions—one can imagine installations on the killing of doctors that took place by pro-life fanatics, explorations of what is and isn't a fetus and so on.

Rancière is certainly *not* supportive of Badiou's position, levying three charges against inaesthetics (2004a). I will review all three criticisms since they raise profound questions for radical pedagogy. Rancière maintains that the true sense of democracy and politics occurs when the dominant 'police order' is reconfigured, and thus there is a redistribution of the sensible: 'the part that has no part' becomes visible, boisterous, and there is a redivision of space and time (Rancière, 2004b). The aesthetics of politics is therefore all about what is art and what is non-art; for example, is popular culture art, or must a categorical line be draw? This is a political issue when it comes to the re-distribution of sensibility. Rancière's concern for the re-distribution of the sensible is confined to the 'police order', what Badiou calls the situation. Democratic rupture in the 'state' would lead to a 'different count'. Badiou's concern for the event means that the new aesthetic that is affirmed exceeds the police order as the state of the situation and *not* from the distribution of the sensible. Hence, as Shaw (2007, p. 192) argues, Rancière's first criticism that the relation between art and non-art is reinstated by Badiou's reascribing a 'propriety' to art is off the mark.

Rancière's second criticism is similar in claiming that inaesthetics supports a modernism that guarantees art's autonomy while denying its heteronomy, which leads to 'aesthetic indistinction' and again fails to socially redistribute sensibility. Inaesthetics, for Rancière, continues to quietly police the frontiers of art and non-art by reinstating the separabilty of the arts (as mimesis) to allow for subtraction. As Shaw (p. 193) argues, this criticism does not hold either given that what is 'proper' to art is a truth or Idea, which is never confined to just one work but constitutes its configuration of multiple works. One work can never imitate or represent (mime) the Idea. An artistic configuration does not *represent* truth; it is but one instance of the procedure that retains its fidelity to the event. Further, Shaw suggests that modernism should not be totally dismissed. Inaesthetics is *not* a totalizing philosophy of art. Intraphilosophy engages in *some* works that are ruptures of previous configurations. Given the situation of designer capitalism that has blurred the art/non-art distinction since Pop Art, mixing high and low forms of art, perhaps the space of autonomy that has been lost to the market is precisely what is needed to remain political—a position that Adorno maintained. This seems also to be Badiou's position—to secure artistic configurations worthy of thought in a globalized world of capitalist consumerism.[15] Rancière's last point is one of concession where he thinks that 'perhaps' inaesthetics, by thinking novelty of events and the fidelity to artistic configurations, is able to break with the previous state of art. Shaw, however, points out that Rancière changed his mind in the version published in *Malaise dans l'esthétique*. Why?

Rancière claimed that Badiou's 15 theses once again reaffirms the 'propriety of art'. But, and this is perhaps crucial to what will follow in my last section, for this charge 'does not exhaust the effects of art', as Shaw maintains (2007, p. 197). Inaesthetics is *privileged* but Badiou addresses art under other conditions of philosophy in his other books as well. More specifically, while inaesthetics is concerned with the reconfiguration between art and non-art, both Badiou and Ranciere argue against any submission of art under ethics—as a Levinasian call of the Other. The event is not guaranteed by the transcendence of God; the infinity of the event is not based on transcendental power but wagered by the subject and the void of the Real as 'the banal reality of every situation' (Badiou in Shaw, p. 196).

Why Art Can't Be Taught—It Can However Educate!

What are the consequences for art and its education given Badiou's inaesthetics? For Badiou, 'Art is pedagogical for the simple reason that it produces truths and because "education" (save in its oppressive and perverted expressions) has never meant anything but this: to arrange the forms of knowledge in such a way that some truth may come to pierce a hole in them' (IN, p. 9). The wager is that art *teaches* truth, or more modestly, *some* art can do this—those *rare* artistic configurations that subtract themselves from a situation thereby punching out the potentiality of a whole new conceptual domain to articulate a new artistic truth. It seems odd to me that Badiou's inaesthetic conceptualism has not been tied to posthuman thought in general given its orientation to the potential 'something else' that breaks with the closed circuit of designer capitalism where the divide between art and non-art has all but disappeared, leaving art to make its presence felt through the spectacularizations of outrageous body performances and installations, blockbuster exhibitions and Biennales? Badiou's inaesthetic conceptualism should be identified as such, *as one potential, certainly a privileged line of flight* away from designer capitalism. What is odder still is Badiou's failure to pay any debt to Deleuze by distancing himself from Deleuze's vitalist realm of *aisthetics*[16] of 'becoming' through a logic of sensation, presumably because it is a dead end in the search for this 'third possibility'. Yet, this inaesthetic 'third possibility', characterized as being *singular and immanent* in its *inventions* (IN, p. 11), being the mirror opposite of Deleuzian *aisthetics*, which is sustained at the level of appearances, cannot entirely do away with the ground of sensibility. If Deleuzian aesthetics 'crawl' with sensibility, Badiou's inaesthetics can leave one cold, puzzled, inattentive and unaffected. That is the danger of asymptotic purification.

It seems to me that this is one of Badiou's major failings; namely, that his search for a 'way out' of designer capitalism by forwarding conceptualist art is simply the other side of the Deleuzian problematic. The difference being that Badiou is *theorizing* the accomplishment of *truth* of the artistic configuration *after the fact*, while Deleuze struggles with the artistic event itself, as it unfolds. Badiou recognizes 'becoming' as a subtractive process, but he is unable to describe it as anything more than as an accomplishment through each 'subject point' in its *post-evental* dimensions. This is why Badiou is so weak speaking to the pre-evental realm as Johnston (2007a,b) has argued, which is where we 'hear' Deleuze and pay attention to him concerning artistic becoming. Pedagogically speaking, with Deleuze one must say, 'art cannot be taught'[17] for this is a realm of creative experimentation characterized by failure, error and accident, which directly bears on 'life' where contingency, uncertainty, ambiguity, paradox and aporias inform it (jagodzinski, 2008a). However, this is not a fall back to a position of Kantian *genius* or *charisma*. No. This is to recognize sensitivity *within* the artistic processes of experimentation that manifest themselves as surprises (pre-evental occurrences) *after the fact*, always in the future anterior and then worked with further by the artist's own sensibilities. There is no 'method' as much, but an approach. Further, artists do not *immediately* know whether they are onto a path of truth in Badiou's terms, for such an unfolding process requires not only fidelity but also *risk* itself. These pre-evental processes are characterized by a particular *schizophrenia* whereby artists must 'split' themselves from work within the situation and pursue artistic creativity that itself is not part of the situation, like Da Vinci's mirrored writings and drawing in his notebooks which would have meant heresy if found by the Church Fathers, or like Jean-François Millet painting Barbizon peasants while still exhibiting in the French Academy.

Creativity, which cannot be *counted*, is therefore continually squeezed out of schooling with its over-emphasis on accountability and evaluation. The gap between art and design is eroding as design begins to strangle creativity by appropriating the same rhetoric of creativity, freedom and self-determination to further the innovation of products for industry.[18] In its experimental forms of pre-eventual becoming—a 'logic of sensation' is at work, the result of which *then* leads to Badiou's notion of truth, the post-eventual dimension of accomplished subtraction. Here, we might say, 'Art can *teach* us that "something new" as truth', the overriding proposition of Badiou's pedagogy. Art has *then* become a certain form of 'knowledge' *for* the world.

Ideally, a new pedagogy of art and its education requires a DeleuzeGuattarian-Badiou assemblage on whose shadow is cast, of course, the Lacanian Real. Here, it must be added that Žižek's (2004) differentiation between Lacan and Badiou over what constitutes the Real cannot be supported for an artistic pedagogy that accounts for its void in the processes of art-ing. It is far too divisive in its contrast. In a nutshell, Žižek maintains that the Real for Lacan is the absolute limit of human experience, which cannot be traversed to impose a new order. Doing so establishes yet another fiction and not a truth. The '*Weiderkehr* experience' with the Real offers insight in the abyss of Being, but no more than that. In distinction, Badiou maintains that the ideal of the truth procedure is never achieved fully. One might say that these are 'gifts' that are added to the world as a result of fidelity to go beyond the situation. As van Rompaey (2006) puts it, 'In other words, that which is articulated or enacted in the *name* of the truth must necessarily be distinguished from the same truth *at the moment of its subjective apprehension*' (p. 355, author's emphasis), which, presumably then becomes a matheme and thereby part of the ontological structure. By far the most sophisticated responses to Žižek's charges against Badiou comes from Bosteels (2005) who attempts to sort out Žižek's enormous influence on the reception of Badiou in Anglophone scholarship.

Posthuman inaesthetic conceptualism, if I have Badiou right, does away with the importance of the artist, strengthens the *logics* of the process, de-aesthetizes and desublimates the art 'object', de-commodifies and makes it 'worthless', difficult to 'sell', and generally de-skills the processes or elevates DIY. The value of crudity as opposed to refinement in terms of the sought for affect is valued more, as is the value of the Idea 'forcing' thought. This is not to say that the initial crudity of working out the trace doesn't become refined, merely that there are many discards as the processes goes on. Conceptualism as a 'subject–point' struggles with 'formalizing the formless' that remains invisible or non-existent to the state (police state, Empire, designer capital). Such works necessarily take place on the border of the void and are monstrous or formless in this sense. There is a growing body of art works that are politicized in this direction. The politically charged works of Alfredo Jaar, Krzysztof Wodiczko, Jochen Gerz, Santiago Serra[19] and Luc Boltanski as forming a particular artistic configuration that speaks *for* the invisible aspects of globalized capitalism, paradoxically by the *silence* they engender as the impossible void is exposed. These artists, or rather the processes that they orchestrate and put into play—what I call *in(design)* (jagodzinski, forthcoming), should be pedagogically studied as 'truth effects'. In this sense we *learn* from them as witnesses-cum-participants. Spectatorship is ruined.

Such a 'machinic' aesthetic is however quintessentially Deleuzian. It is a shift to not what art *means*, but what the *art does and sets into motion*—a Deleuzian problematic. It is arts performative aspect—the intensities of its affects in terms of what they set to accomplish *for* the world. Immanent *aesthetics* as explored through the processes of in(design) in this regard *are an affective deterritorialization*; a becoming that has everything to do with 'life' and not death. Such a position has affinities with Rancière's aesthetics as well in its potential reconfiguration of the sensible. Deleuze and Guattari speak to this much more eloquently than Badiou since their feel for sensibility far exceeds his tendencies towards the matheme. The body in Badiou remains underdeveloped, especially in his inaesthetics of dance as Lewis (2007) maintains.

The occurrence of a 'true' event is rare in the arts. Its impact is characterized in the Lacanian sense as an encounter with the Real. Such an encounter is singular and the artistic body of works that emerge to articulate its trace among many artists require time to co-ordinate. Badiou is clear on this—the 'time' of the event cannot be specified. It is an emergent process. Since all this happens in the future anterior such a pedagogy cannot be taught as a methodology; what artistic pedagogy can do is learn how artists (singular, cell, community) are in tune to the traces of this encounter with the Real of the event that is singular and immanent to them, and them alone. When this tact is taken the *figural dimension* of the BwO plays a much more dominant role at the molecular level, to which Deleuze and Guattari sensitize us more so than does Badiou. The figural level presents us with a 'diagrammatics' in Deleuze's terms, that begins to get at the intuitive emerging of unconscious *sub-signs* that artists work with—the marks and unique subgraphemes, as intensities that are governed by various speeds of the hand that point to an amorphous or unformed space shown by 'anexact' diagrams or pregeometric figures. This is the working of the molecular figural where a back and forth between artist and the emergent work take place. Badiou (2006b) gets at some of this process in his 'Drawing' essay, but not much.

Realistically, it is the experience of the psychic Real on lesser levels (an *encounter* in Deleuzian terms) than Badiou's *proper event* as such which Deleuze and Guattari theorize, since the strength of the fidelity to the event depends on how strongly one is affected. The various 'subject-points' that emerge in the post-eventical dimension must continually 'point back' to the traces of the event as a process that is self-refleXive in its trace of identifiable sequences as subject-points. I have been using the term self-refleXive (jagodzinski, 2008b) as opposed to self-reflection or self-reflexivity, to get at the 'X' referring to the fidelity of the event itself. As an encounter with the Real (*Wiederkehr*) this means to grasp the emerging sub-signs at the unconscious molecular dimensions of creation. I offer one example by Elizabeth Murray an artist whose cancer got the better of her, passing on in 2007. As she says of her process, 'For a couple of years I've been working with cutting out shapes and kind of grouping them together and letting it go where it may. Like basically making a zigzag shape and making a rectangular shape and a circular bloopy fat cloud shape and just putting them all together and sort of letting the cards fall where they may. And I don't know why I am doing it this way ... The thing that has been hard about these paintings is that I don't know how I am going to get them resolved. Its like the resolution has to happen without anybody seeing it, not even me' (Murray, *Art 21*). Murray is referring to the future anterior effects and the way her unconscious/conscious affects are playing off each other, an example of self-refleXivity. Murray's sculptural paintings do offer a 'truth' of sorts in the way different shapes dynamically co-exist with one another in their heterogeneity.

Pedagogically, what Murray is doing cannot be taught. She is intuitively feeling the traces of the event (of which she is no idea as to where it will lead) to develop her affective body of subject-points. Pedagogy would need to further this non-rational ordering of the inform as form. In brief, the stress would shift from the current emphasis on 'making' (*praxis*) to 'doing' (*poesis*); that is to say the 'doing' emphasizes 'becoming' as a fidelity with the *encounter* with 'object' of art (the object is not necessarily material) that is characterized by self-refleXivity as an unconscious intuitive process of art-ing, theorized as a gerund and more broadly as processes of in(design). There is 'risk' involved since failure is part of such procedure that develops subjectivity, as Lacan would have it, as a future anterior 'happening'.

In summary, art and its education for Badiou's 'third possibility' that challenges designer capitalism would consist of a Deleuze-Badiou assemblage underwritten by the Lacanian Real that adequately recognizes both the pre-evental and post-evental subject-points. Such a potential for actualization cannot happen in schooling as it presently structured, nor in art schools where design for global capitalism is supplanting the once established realm of freedom of art as historically opened up by German Idealism. Perhaps the *sites* of community art as developed by a number of the artists I have mentioned, who are forming the configuration of subject-points of an emerging truth about global capitalism should be the line of flight we educators follow.

Notes

1. Two of the most significant have been transcribed and made available online in *The Symptom* and *Lacanian Ink* as 'The Subject of Art' and 'Fifteen Theses on Contemporary Art' respectively. Oddly, Badiou's Fifteen Theses, published as 'Manifesto of Affirmationism', does not appear in this commentary. They date from December 2003 and can be found in English as translated by Peter Hallward at http://www.lacan.com/frameXXIII7.htm. 'Arts Imperative: Speaking the unspeakable' (2006a) exists as a webcast recording at the Drawing Center, NYC delivered on March 8, 2006 that appears as a slightly modified essay called 'Drawing', which is a meditation on art as a 'description without place' based on a poem by Wallace Stevens.
2. See the discussion concerning the performance of Lucas Murgida posted on the *Perverse Egalitarianism* blog under 'Badiou and Performance Art: Some Notes'. Available at http://pervegalit.wordpress.com/2007/11/27/badiou-and-performance-art/
3. In my own work I use the homonym site/sight/cite for the three Lacanian registers respectively as Real/Imaginary/Symbolic. Here the 'site' of the Real as a void identifies precisely Badiou's characterization of contemporary art as 'description without place' (Drawing, p. 43). An installation is the new place that displaces all things in it. It describes the relationship between things that are outside their 'normal' place and relationship. Duchamp's 'readymades' stage the first installation as the initial event.
4. The French sensible means, like the English 'sensible', 'perceptible by the senses', but it does not carry the English overtones of 'well-reasoned' or 'making good sense'. It is better rendered as 'sensorial', 'sensate', 'phenomenal', or 'sense-able' (Laura Balladur, fn. 1, p. 154, in During, 2005).

5. On the notion of the 'formless' see Bois and Krauss's (1997) theorizations on an exhibition of the same name.

6. Much like a symptom that has to return twice to be acknowledged, the first time it is repressed and not registered, the second time remembered, I follow the distinction Lacan (1988) makes in S XI between *Wiederkehr* and *Wiederholung*. The first is simply repetition, while the second is repetition with a difference.

7. I turn to the insights offered by During (2005) who is contra Badiou in relation to Rancière, and Shaw (2007) who is pro Badiou is relation to Rancière to see me through this section. However, the strong Lacanian bent will be maintained.

8. Famously presented as the discourse of the Master, University, Hysteric and the Analyst.

9. Lacan's discourses of the Master, University, Hysteric and Analyst are developed in his 1969–70 seminars, Book XVII: The Other Side of Psychoanalysis (2006).

10. The didactic (Platonic) schema produces an instrumental truth in art as semblance or appearance that is external to it in relation to the social Good; while with the hermeneutic (Romantic) schema, truth is internal to art via the sensible manifestation of *Geist* as in Hegel; in the classical (Aristotelian) schema the truth of art is through its cathartic effects. All three aesthetic positions fall under ethics, whereas inaesthetics presents truth as thinking itself as an effect that engages in the transformation of the situation in line with new forms of egalitarian principles. It is not established but created knowledge, generating a new truth.

11. During (2005, pp. 146–149) illustrates the inaesthetic through Mallarmé, Badiou's principle exemplar. Unfortunately, I have no 'feel' for his poetry.

12. Badiou articulates his plea for an 'affirmationist art' in 2001 at a conference held in Venice called 'The Question of Art in the Third Millennium', which was subsequently published in 2003. A shortened version of his position can be found in *Polemics* (2006c).

13. Rancière's critique of Badiou was first presented at a conference dedicated to Badiou in 1999. It was then published in *Alain Badiou: Penser le multiple* in 2002, further revised and included in his *Malaise dans l'esthétique*. There is an English translation that appeared in Hallward's edited volume, *Think Again* (2004a). However, as Shaw (2007, pp. 195–196) informs us, his essay in *Malaise dans l'esthétique* has a far more detrimental conclusion. Rancière's rather unsuccessful critique of Deleuzian aesthetics can be found in *Qui Parle* (Rancière, 2004c).

14. In *What is Philosophy?* (1994), within the section, 'Percept, Affect, and Concept', they state that 'the work of art is a *being of sensation* and nothing else; it exists in itself' (p. 164, emphasis added).

15. Shaw cleverly points out that Rancière has normalized his third historical paradigm—'the aesthetic regime'—with the ruination of the hierarchies of art by confusing art and non-art categories towards 'progressive' egalitarian ends. However, he forgets that this blurring may no longer be politically useful and that another regime of art in the future can continue to practice a politics of dissensus.

16. I will continue to use the Greco-Latin term for sensibility/sensations in their unformed or informed state rather than aesthetics, which already indicates their containment through stylized form through human praxis.

17. I borrow this aphorism from Elkins (2001) whose makes the same case somewhat differently within art schools across the country. Art, however, can be taught when it comes to designer capitalism. There is no shortage of the way innovations do happen.

18. I have dealt with this issue elsewhere (jagodzinski, 2006b). See also Beatrice von Bismarck (2005) who argues the same in the German literature.

19. In September 2002 invitations were sent out to members of the art scene to attend the opening of the £500,000 extension of the Lisson Gallery on Bell Street in London. When the guest turned up expecting champagne and canapés, what they found instead was that the whole front gallery had been boarded up by a large expanse of corrugated iron, with no means of entrance. The guests were at first puzzled at being shut out. Finally, the artist

Santiago Sierra turned up and told them that this was the exhibit called Closed Space by Corrugated Metal. Sierra was quoted in the Guardian as saying, 'It was part of a broader work which is a commentary on the frustration at not being able to get in somewhere for economic or political reasons'. Sierra is directly addressing the society of synoptic control.

References

Badiou, A. (2003) Beyond Formalism: An Interview (with Bruno Bosteels and Peter Hallward), B. Bosteels & A. Toscano, trans., *Angelaki: Journal of the Theoretical Humanities*, 8:2, pp. 111–136 [BF in text].

Badiou, A. (2004) Fifteen Theses on Contemporary Art, *Lacanian Ink*, 23, pp. 103–119 [Theses in text].

Badiou, A. (2005a) *Being and Event*, O. Feltham, trans. (London, Continuum) [BE in text].

Badiou, A. (2005b) *Handbook of Inaesthetics*, A. Toscano, trans. (Stanford, CA, Stanford University Press) [IN in text].

Badiou, A. (2005c) The Subject of Art, L. Kerr, transcription, *The Symptom*, 6 (Spring) available at http://www.lacan.com/newspaper6.htm [SA in text].

Badiou, A. (2006a) Arts Imperative: Speaking the unspeakable, Webcast Recording available at http://www.lacan.com/issue26.htm.

Badiou, A. (2006b) Drawing, *Lacanian Ink*, 28, pp. 42–48 [Drawing in text].

Badiou, A. (2006c) Third Sketch of a Manifesto of Affirmationist Art, in: A. Badiou, *Polemics*, S. Corcoran, trans. and introduction (London and New York, Verso), pp. 133–148.

Bois, Y.-A. & Krauss, R. E. (1997) *Formless: A User's Guide* (New York, Zone Books).

Bois, Y.-A., Brett, G., Iversen, M. & Stallbrass, J. (2008) An Interview with Mark Wallinger, *October*, 123 (Winter), pp. 185–204.

Bosteels, B. (2005) Badiou without Žižek, *Polygraph*, 17, pp. 221–244.

Deleuze, G. & Guattari, F. (1994) *What is Philosophy?* H. Tomlinson & G. Burchel, trans. (New York: Columbia University Press).

Deleuze, G. (1990) *The Logic of Sense*, M. Lester & C. Stivale, trans. (New York, Columbia University Press).

During, E. (2005) How Much Truth Can Art Bear? On Badiou's 'inaesthetics', *Polygraph*, 17, pp. 143–155.

Elkins, J. (2001) *Why Art Can't Be Taught: A handbook for art students* (Chicago, University of Chicago Press).

Foster, H. (1996) *The Return of the Real: The avant-garde at the end of the century* (Cambridge, MA, MIT Press).

Hallward, P. (2003) *Badiou: A Subject to Truth* (Minneapolis, University of Minnesota Press).

jagodzinski, j. (2006a) Jacque Lacan as Queer Theorist: Is there a 'beyond' to identification politics in education?, *Journal of Curriculum Theorizing* (Fall), 22:3, pp. 55–70.

jagodzinski, j. (2006b) Without Title: On the impossibility of art education: art as becoming-posthuman [Gaitskell Address, Nov. 24, 2006], *Canadian Journal of Education Through Art*, 5:2, pp. 6–15.

jagodzinski, j. (2008a) Postmetaphysical Vision: Art education's challenge in an age of globalized aesthetics (a mondofesto), *Studies in Art Education*, 49:2, pp. 147–160.

jagodzinski, j. (2008b) *Television and Youth Culture: Televised paranoia* (New York and London, Palgrave).

jagodzinski, j. (forthcoming) Beyond Aesthetics: Returning Force and Truth to Art and Its Education, *Studies in Art Education*.

Johnston, A. (2007a) The Quick and the Dead: Alain Badiou and the split speeds of transformation, *International Journal of Žižek Studies* 1:2 available at http://zizekstudies.org/index.php/ijzs/article/view/28/88.

Johnston, A. (2007b) Addendum: 'Let a Thousand Flowers Bloom!'—Some brief remarks on and responses to Žižek's 'Badiou: Notes from an ongoing debate', *International Journal of Žižek Studies*, 1:2 available at http://zizekstudies.org/index.php/ijzs/article/view/27/87.

Lacan, J. (1988) *Four Fundamental Concepts of Psycho-analysis*, J.-A. Miller, ed.; A. Sheridan, trans. (London, Vintage).

Lacan, J. (2006) *The Seminar of Jacques Lacan: Book XVII: The other side of psychoanalysis*, R. Grigg, trans. (New York, W.W. Norton).

Lang, B. (1982) Looking for the Styleme, *Critical Inquiry*, 9:2 (December), pp. 405–413.

Lewis, T. (2007) Philosophy—Aesthetics—Education: Reflections on Dance, *Journal of Aesthetic Education*, 41:4, pp. 53–66.

Ling, A. (2006) Can Cinema be Thought?: Alain Badiou and the artistic condition, *Cosmos and History: The Journal of Natural and Social Philosophy*, 2:1–2, pp. 263–276.

Murray, E. *Art 21*, available at http://www.pbs.org/art21/.

Rancière, J. (2004a) Aesthetics, Inaesthetics, anti-aesthetics, in: P. Hallward (ed.), *Think Again: Alain Badiou and the future of philosophy* (London and New York, Continuum), pp. 218–237.

Rancière, J. (2004b) *The Politics of Aesthetics: The distribution of the sensible*, G. Rockhill, trans. and intro. (London and New York, Continuum).

Rancière, J. (2004c) Is There a Deleuzian Aesthetics?, *Qui Parle*, 14:2, pp. 1–14.

Shaw, D. Z. (2007) Inaesthetics and Truth: The debate between Alain Badiou and Jacques Rancière, *Filozofski Vestnik*, 28:2, pp. 183–202.

van Rompaey, C. (2006) Book Review: A question of fidelity, *Cosmos and History: The Journal of Natural and Social Philosophy*, 2:1–2, pp. 350–358.

von Bismarck, B. (ed.) (2005) *Grenzbespielungen: Visuelle Politik in der Übergangzone* (Cologne, Verlag der Büchandlung König).

Žižek, S. (2004) From Purification to Subtraction: Badiou and the Real, in: P. Hallward (ed.), *Think Again: Alain Badiou and the future of philosophy* (London and New York, Continuum), pp. 165–181.

4
Alain Badiou, Jacques Lacan and the Ethics of Teaching

Peter M. Taubman

> There is no ethics in general. (Alain Badiou, 2001, p. 16)
> The only thing one can be guilty of is giving ground relative to one's desire. (Jacques Lacan, 1992, p. 319)
> There is no safety. (James Baldwin, interview, March 1987)

Introduction

This chapter addresses the following questions: What constitutes an ethics of teaching? What, as teachers, should our ethical response be to events that radically disturb our and our students' identities, beliefs and relationships? What might an ethics of teaching look like, when we encounter in ourselves and in our students emotional states ignored in standard curricula or in everyday discussions or when we face extraordinary events that resist easy symbolization or when we confront what Lacan called the Real?

In order to explore these questions I turn to the work of Alain Badiou, specifically his *Ethics: An essay on the understanding of evil*, and of his teacher, Jacques Lacan, both of whom have understood ethics as a response to or encounter with that which may be potentially life altering—for Lacan the 'Real', for Badiou the 'event'. I employ insights from Badiou's theory of ethics, along with Lacan's understanding of ethics, to critique mainstream approaches to pedagogical ethics and to limn an alternative ethics of teaching. Along the way, I raise questions and concerns about Badiou's theory of ethics, which seem to me to reveal a yearning for revolutionary commitment contradicted by his recoil from the suffering that can be justified in the name of a principle.

Badiou's Ethics

As the epigram at the opening of this chapter suggests, Badiou, like Lacan, rejects ethics conceived in terms of a general rule, a set of norms, or an *a priori* set of principles that regulates our relationships or actions. Badiou and Lacan both view this normalizing approach to ethics as potentially leading to terrorism because it imposes on everyone the particularity of a few. Following Lacan, Badiou writes, 'There is no ethics in general' (Badiou, 2001, p. 16); '[e]thics does not exist. There is only the ethic-of (of politics, of love, of science, of art)' (Badiou, 2001, p. 28), or as Lacan would say, of psychoanalysis.

For both Badiou and Lacan ethics has to do with an encounter with the Real, or:

> ... those limit-experiences in which the subject finds himself confronted with ... the 'night of the world', the self-withdrawal, the absolute contradiction of subjectivity, the severing of links with 'reality'. (Žižek quoted in Hallward, 2001, xviii)

For Lacan, the Real has several connotations, ranging from the unconscious to that which is beyond symbolization to the traumatic kernel of one's being (see Ragland, 1996, pp. 192–211). For our purposes we can understand it as the un-nameable against which symbolization falters (Lacan, 1988, p. 66), or as the un-assimilated horror that can irrupt in and reveal the incompleteness or cracks in our taken-for-granted identity or reality (Žižek, 1994, p. 29). Ethical choice emerges when one is faced with that which threatens to destabilize one's world, one's situation. In the normal course of things, we simply go our own way, ordinary humans, driven hither and thither by what Badiou calls 'opinions' and 'bureaucratic routine' and 'our animal humanity' and what Lacan calls the 'service of goods' (Badiou, 2001, p. 80). But occasionally, we encounter the Real, 'something which cannot be calculated, predicted or managed' (Badiou, 2001, pp. 122–123), something which disturbs the taken-for-granted coordinates of our daily lives and sense of who we are. It is in that particular situation, that we are confronted with what both Badiou and Lacan term ethics.

Perhaps a quote from James Baldwin would be of some help in beginning to understand this confrontation with the Real or what Badiou will theorize as the event. We can think of the terror that Baldwin refers to in the following quote as arising in the moment of an encounter with the Real.

> [T]his terror has something to do with the irreducible gap between the self one invents—the self one takes oneself as being, which is, however, and by definition a provisional self—and the undiscoverable self, which always has the power to blow the provisional self to bits. It is perfectly possible to discover ... the self one has sewn together with such effort ... is gone: and out of what raw material will one build a self again? (Baldwin, 1985, p. 383)

While neither Badiou nor Lacan posit the agentic individual Baldwin's quote implies, both would see in such an encounter and the gap it opens the ethical possibility. For both these men, and for Baldwin in his own way, that ethic is defined in terms of allegiance to one's truth or the truth of the situation. For Baldwin, it is the truth of living in the gap and acknowledging the precariousness and contingency of one's history, one's self and one's identity. For Lacan, it is the truth of desire. But for Badiou, it is the truth of the event and faithfulness to that truth. 'A crisis of fidelity is always what puts to the test, following the collapse of an image, the sole maxim of consistency (and thus ethics): Keep going!' (Badiou, 2001, p. 79). Keep being faithful to one's truth. In the face of the terror Baldwin describes, confronted with the Lacanian Real, or faced with the irruption of the event, we must keep living the truth of new provisional selves rather than retreating to older fixed ones (Baldwin), must not give ground on our desire (Lacan), must remain faithful to the consequences of the irruption of the event and keep going (Badiou).

But what is this truth of which Badiou speaks? It is not a universal Truth in the traditional sense, nor does it refer to an individual's subjective truth in the sense of 'Well, that's *my* opinion'. Striving to resuscitate the idea of truth, an idea that has been discredited by poststructuralists' attacks on metaphysics and because of its deployment as a justification for violence and oppression, Badiou argues that truth exists always and only as *a singular* truth that emerges when what he labels a 'situation' becomes an event and when one commits to the truth of the event. This needs some explanation.

Peter Hallward, in his introduction to *Ethics: An essay on the understanding of evil*, simplifies Badiou's understanding of human affairs this way:

> Badiou divides the sphere of human action into two overlapping but sharply differentiated sub-spheres: (a) the ordinary realm of established interests and differences, of approved knowledges that serve to name, recognize and place consolidated identities, and (b) an exceptional realm of singular innovations or truths, which persists only through the militant proclamation of those rare individuals who constitute themselves as the subjects of a truth, as the militants of their cause. (Hallward, 2001, p. viii)

There exists on one hand the status quo, what Badiou calls the 'state' of the situation, which consists of our quotidian lives—dogmatic opinions, institutionalized knowledges, habits, bureaucratic allegiances, and the pursuit of fulfilling our animal appetites. It is, if you will, the conditioned life, the doxa, or, in psychoanalytic terms, the un-examined, overdetermined life. Badiou intentionally uses 'state' to suggest the role the State plays in maintaining this status quo. On the other hand there is what Badiou calls 'subjective truth', which only emerges when a situation suddenly, as if by chance, or what Badiou will call grace, shifts, revealing what had, until that moment, been a void in the situation. This shift reveals what had always been there but had remained invisible, until a subject commits to the consequences of the event, allowing that event to unfold as the truth of the situation. Badiou argues that only if we commit to the truth of the event, remain faithful to its consequences, can we avoid corruption, and only by committing to that truth do we transcend our conditioned, overdetermined lives, becoming our better or what he calls 'Immortal' self. But what is an event and what is its truth?

Badiou describes an event as 'a hazardous ... unpredictable supplement to the situation ... . [which] brings to pass "something other" than the situation' (2001, p. 67). The event is immanent to a situation, but is not part of it. Before it becomes an event through the subject's commitment to the consequences of the event, the event exists only as a void in the situation. The 'void', according to Badiou, is at 'the heart of a situation' but 'remains unnamed' until, through a person's commitment to the event, 'the not-known of the situation' (2001, pp. 68–9) is re-named, thus changing the situation. Before it has been re-named, the event is meaningless according to the prevailing language and established knowledge of the situation. It emerges as a truth event simultaneously with the subject's commitment to the event and naming of it, and in turn the subject comes into being with that naming. Hallward writes, 'A truth comes into being through those subjects who maintain a resilient fidelity to the consequences of an event that took place in a situation but was not of it' (2001, p. x).

Badiou suggests that what raises us out of the status quo, our 'situation', what raises us from 'our animal nature' to what he calls the 'Immortal man' is the 'event' and our fidelity to its consequences. Such an event makes us, through our commitment, a subject.

> [A] subject ... needs something to have happened, something that cannot be reduced to its ordinary inscription in 'what there is' [the state of things]. Let us call this supplement an event ... which compels us to decide a new way of being. (Badiou, 2001, p. 41)

As Kathleen Kesson (2007) puts it, 'When one becomes caught up in an event, there is a loss of self—the small, ego-centered self is literally taken over by something larger than the self' (p. 2). One's ontological coordinates shift in the process of experiencing the event and committing to its consequences, and one becomes, through that commitment, a subject.

As I understand him, Badiou is claiming that in a given state there are multiple possibilities. When, by chance, an irruption within the situation occurs and someone is seized by that irruption an event becomes possible. As that someone commits to the truth of the event, renaming it and the situation, which, retroactively re-named, now comes into being in a different form, that someone becomes a subject or 'Immortal' for as long as the commitment is held. The subject for Badiou exists as a fusion between a human animal and a principle or cause or idea or passion or artistic endeavor constitutive of a specific event. Two associations come to mind here that may help us understand Badiou's assertions.

First is Kuhn's (1962) idea of a paradigm shift. A rupture or break in the given situation produced by what was in that situation but not acknowledged within it (the void) is adhered to by those who come to rearticulate, rename or re-conceptualize the older paradigm and thus through their fidelity to the new paradigm not only change the older state of things and produce what will become a new situation but also in their commitment to the consequences of this rupture, become other than who they were. As Kesson (2007) writes, 'This truth process is akin to a paradigm shift; it reflects a theory of transformation that illuminates how the ordinary and the habitual might be superseded by something else—a something that was absent in the prior situation or existed as potential in what Badiou calls the void' (p. 3).

My second association is to the way psychoanalytic understanding arrives through a commitment to the transferential relationship with the analyst. Only after we are committed to an analysis, that is, only after the transference has taken hold, does our understanding of who we have been and are slowly arrive. The analysand, encountering the Real of the unconscious through the transference, gradually emerges from the overdetermined patterns, opinions, knowledge that constituted the analysand's ontological moorings, and, in the process, the analysand emerges as a subject. Coming to us through the transference, psychoanalytic understanding shifts our ontological and epistemological coordinates. In interpreting the transference we rearticulate or rename who we were and thus shift our current situation and become other than we were. The transference results from, if you will, a lived but unconscious commitment to the analysis, and results in a truth event that will have changed one's situation and retrospectively changed one's interpretation of the past.

Let's take an example of the event and the truth of which Badiou speaks, from one of Badiou's four truth conditions, which constitute for him modes of access to the Absolute: politics, art, science (mathematics) and love. In terms of politics the French Revolution of 1792 or the Civil Rights movement of 1955 would name truth events. In each, incidents led to individuals risking and in a sense relinquishing their position in the situation to become, through their fidelity to the emergent truth processes, part of a movement and revolution. In that commitment those individuals not only renamed the event as a truth process that would become the Movement or Revolution but also re-conceptualized the situation and emerged as subjects. In each case, what was considered impossible, what was not even acknowledged, became possible. As Badiou writes, '[E]mancipatory politics always consists in making seem possible precisely that which, from within the situation, is declared to be impossible' (Badiou, 2001, p. 121).

But what does it mean to be faithful to an event? In part it implies 'an effectively selfless devotion to a cause' (Hallward, 2001, p. xi). It also means 'thinking the situation according to the event' (Badiou, 2001, p. 41). In other words, to use one of the above examples, it means thinking of the extant situation in the American south in the mid-1950s in the new terms opened up by the bus boycott and mobilization, and most importantly in terms of visible cracks and openings in the state of things. To be really faithful to an event means 'completely rework[ing] my ordinary way of living my situation' (Badiou, 2001, p. 42). It means, as Badiou puts it, sounding similar to Baldwin, not giving 'up on that part of yourself that you do not know' and 'seiz[ing] in your being that which has seized and broken you' (Badiou, 2001, p. 47).

Before I turn to my own disquiet with Badiou's ethics and discuss how both Badiou and Lacan can complicate our thinking about the ethics of teaching, I want to go just a bit further into Badiou's theory of ethics. While the Good in Badiou's ethics consists of allegiance to a particular truth process arising when an event occurs, the potential for Evil emerges, according to Badiou, at the same moment. It does not precede the Good. It is not some massified entity, some radical evil that exists autonomously in the world. Nor does it have anything to do with distance from the Good. Rather it has three components: terror, betrayal, and disaster. Badiou writes,

For Evil has three names:
- to believe that an event convokes not the void of the earlier situation but its plenitude, is Evil in the sense of *simulacrum* or *terror*;
- to fail to live up to a fidelity is Evil in the sense of *betrayal*, betrayal in oneself of the Immortal that you are;

- to identify a truth with total power is Evil in the sense of *disaster*. (Badiou, 2001, p. 71, italics in original)

Let us consider these in terms of the Baldwin quote above and in terms of the Civil Rights movement. Faced with the choice of returning to what was a former self or situation, or forming a new self, choosing evil, that is choosing terror and mistaking the *simulacrum* for the truth would consist of refashioning a self on old ways, according to old values and elevating these to a truth for everyone. For example, the minister, who shattered by an exposed affair, returns more certain than ever of the sinfulness of adultery and blames homosexuals for the decline in morality, or the educator who, appalled by the suffering in Iraq, the Sudan and Nigeria, locates all evil in the Bush/Cheney administration, scolds his students for not attending enough to global horrors, and continues to drive an SUV—these are examples of those who choose the plenitude rather than the void. In other words they simply rearrange what was, rather than encounter the void of Baldwin's question and commit to answering it, however long such an effort might take.

In terms of the Civil Rights movement, those whites and blacks who lambasted King and Baldwin for not supporting taking up arms against whites, and located evil in whites *per se* as opposed to structures of inequality and prejudice, rearranged the extant situation, re-naming not the void, but the plenitude. They simply flipped the occupiers of structurally pre-given positions. These individuals have chosen a *simulacrum* of the truth process; have chosen terror. And terror arises *out of* a failure to see one's own complicity in the situation and *from* a decision made in the service of the few rather than all.

The second evil Badiou describes is *betrayal*. The person who for a moment was captivated by or inspired to commit to a principle or cause but who failed to see it through, or the lover who betrays his passion by turning the beloved back into just-a-regular person, or worse an intoxicant who has temporarily blinded the lover, that person betrays the event and in Badiou's eyes chooses evil.

> This explains why former revolutionaries are obliged to declare that they used to be lost in error and madness, why a former lover no longer understands why he loved that woman, why a tired scientist comes to misunderstand, and to frustrate through bureaucratic routine, the very development of his own science. Since the process of truth is an immanent break, you can leave it only by breaking with this break which has seized you. (Badiou, 2001, pp. 79–80)

Finally, the third evil, *disaster*, results when we use a particular truth to totalize all phenomena. From such a perspective, a Civil Rights movement transformed into Black power advocating black supremacy was not only destructive to the movement but was much safer within the situation of white supremacy than a poor people's campaign, which threatened the class structure. Furthermore, to lose oneself totally in any cause or to any principle or to any identity is to totalize oneself rather than allow the multiple parts of oneself to flourish. '[E]very attempt to impose the total power of truth ruins that truth's foundation' (Badiou,

2001, p. 84), even if that truth is the truth of racial or cultural or sexual identity. Such an attempt only strengthens the fiction of the ego, rather than loosening its hold. Thus, the subject emerging with the evental truth of the Civil Rights movement and with a fidelity to the consequences of that movement, opens the way for disaster, if, rather than remaining faithful to the truth of that movement, it trumpets the positivity of Blackness as a totalizing identity, whose definition and sphere of action maintains the Whiteness/Blackness categories of the State or situation.

Three Concerns about Badiou's Ethics

With this all too brief summary of Badiou's thoughts on ethics, I want to turn to three concerns I have with Badiou's understanding of ethics. The first centers on how Badiou distinguishes between a *simulacrum* and an authentic truth event. Let me provide an example of what concerns me. It is not clear to me how Badiou's ethics of commitment to a particular truth would not include the Bush administration's policy in Iraq. If we think of 9/11 as constituting an event for the administration, one which they renamed as the war on terror, the war for democratizing the Middle East and the movement to bring democracy for all, and one whose dire consequences they have been faithful to no matter what the cost materially, psychically or politically, can we not consider this an authentic event rather than a *simulacrum*? The very fact that the truth-process has not ended but is endless adds weight to the authenticity of the event. As Seymour Hersh said in a May 2005 Pacifica radio interview, 'Bush is truly a Trotskyite, a believer in permanent revolution'.

The second concern I have takes us back to the Baldwin quote. What is not clear to me is what pieces will be used to create the new. It is one thing to remain loyal to one's decision, but the assumption seems to be that simply by remaining loyal a 'new' emerges. This recalls Sartre's (1947) existential engagement: first you decide and then you figure out the reasons and see what such a commitment allows you to do. While such engagement, which in Badiou's case is grounded in a singular truth, offers a refreshing alternative to the wobbly neoliberal rhetoric of compromise that masks playing it safe and protecting privilege—witness the continued failure of the Democrats to actually assume the progressive or radical position the Right always accuses them of occupying—it offers form as content. In other words, it is an ordinary person's commitment to the truth of an event in which that person's Immortal being is called forth that constitutes Badiou's ethics.

To be fair, Badiou is well aware of his rejection of any general content for ethics. He follows Kant here in draining ethics of any pathological content, although, unlike Kant, he does not set up a normalized ethical form, like duty, and clearly opposes any ethics in general. But because the ethical choice is both constitutive of and consequent to the evental truth, it seems that for Badiou ethics fundamentally consists of finding oneself seized by an event, caught up in a truth-process and committing to the truth emerging from and consequences resulting from that event, whatever they are. On what basis is the new, which eventually will become a new situation, erected? Furthermore, the form of the commitment is unclear. Badiou uses the word 'militant', but does that mean violence? How is commitment measured? For Lacan, it is measured by one's willingness to sacrifice not only one's life but more importantly, one's ontological moorings, or, in other words, one's innermost core of being and one's social standing, but the sacrifice is in the name of understanding one's own desire. Such a Lacanian view of ethics at first glance may seem to cast the current administration's actions as ethical, but on closer inspection, it does not, since it focuses at the level of desire and on taking responsibility for one's own desire and its coordinates as opposed to framing it in terms of what is good for others or in terms of an external reality.

Because Badiou does not locate the truth event at the level of desire, he necessarily falls into the public world of conscious decisions. Thus, I would argue, the pursuit into eternity of the Iraq policy could be seen, from his perspective, as ethical. His caveat that 'The Good is good only to the extent that it does not aspire to render the world good' (Badiou, 2001, p. 85), makes eminent sense to me, but where one draws the boundaries of the world remains unclear. If his caveat means not imposing one's truth on others, but simply following one's choice to the end, Badiou would seem to be calling for a Sartrean (1947) ethics stripped of the reminder that when one chooses, one chooses for everyone. To be fair, Badiou might replace 'everyone' with 'All' and argue that such an empty category would be filled by the most immiserated among us, but this still leaves us with the question of how one decides to fill the category and establish the world's boundaries. If the caveat returns us to ethics as form, an ethical act, however singular, would seem not only to consist of a perpetual revolution, a kind of endless May 1968, but also render it vulnerable to fanaticism.

The third concern I have revolves around Badiou's notion of grace. In other words, how does it happen that one is called to be an Immortal? How does one know when an event is happening? Is it chance? Do we go through life waiting for such grace? Can one prepare for such a moment? Is it everywhere available all the time?

While I have questions about Badiou's ethics, there are important aspects of his theory that I believe can help us identify the shortcomings of mainstream approaches to pedagogical ethics. In particular his definitions of evil and his rejection of an *a priori* evil problematize current approaches to the ethics of teaching. As I shall argue in the concluding section, his insights into ethics and fidelity to an evental truth, when coupled with Lacan's ethics of psychoanalysis, offer an alternative version of pedagogical ethics.

Mainstream Approaches to the Ethics of Teaching

Mainstream approaches to the ethics of teaching, I would argue, are framed in three ways: as a response to an *a priori* evil, as tolerating the Other outside or inside ourselves, and as obeying the law. I want to look at each of these.

Ethics as a Response to an A Priori Evil

Educators often conceive ethics in terms of protecting children from an assortment of dangers, e.g. drugs, promiscuous sex and pregnancy, sexual and physical abuse, and violence. Several of the authors writing in a classic text on early childhood education, *Making a Place for Pleasure in Early Childhood Education*, edited by Joseph Tobin (1997), address this kind of ethics when they discuss the moral panic that often shapes the practices of teachers. Whether the panic is over sexual abuse or promiscuity, drug use or violence, learning disabilities or behavioral problems, intolerance or bias in schools, the response is framed in terms of our ethical responsibility to respond to an *a priori* evil against which we teachers and educators need to defend.

What is the problem with framing pedagogical ethics in this way? What is the problem with basing an ethics on the positing of an *a priori* evil? Following Badiou's discussion of evil, I would suggest that framing ethics as a response to an *a priori* evil has three consequences. First, it defines students and children as victims rather than as agents. It posits their primary identity as something that can be hurt. Constructing children or adolescents this way ties the child or adolescent's goodness to her or his position as victim, as vulnerable to evil. As soon as the child or adolescent no longer behaves like a victim, but wants to claim his or her own desires, resistances, rights, he or she is magically turned into a 'bad kid' or pathologized. One need think only of the disabled child positioned as victim and dependent on the humane services of the special educator. When she or he becomes militant and demands equal access, she or he is positioned as extreme or non-compliant. Or consider gay, lesbian or transgendered students who are tolerated, who benefit perhaps from educational attempts to lessen prejudice in the school, but who become a problem if their overt behavior doesn't conform to the heteronormative ethos of the school. Or consider the attention in schools given to the events of 9/11. Teachers and educators focused on how students were supposedly traumatized or on how students needed to heal or on how students needed to feel a renewed sense of patriotism or on how teachers needed to reassure students that they were safe. One need only imagine the student in elementary school or high school who experienced the attacks in terms of their perfect execution or who claimed that he or she was not particularly moved by what happened or who actually understood the attacks as a political response to US imperialism to realize how quickly they would be pathologized. The Real that irrupted on 9/11 was quickly defined in terms of an *a priori* evil the effects of which on kids needed immediate attention and soothing.

The second problem with positing evil as an *a priori* to be responded to is that the possibility of imagining a transformation of the way things are becomes much more difficult, because all our attention is riveted on an extant evil, its effects, and our responses to it. Our responses to that evil are necessarily shaped by it, just as our thinking about that evil and its effects is shaped by the focus on that evil. Altering the frame such that both evil and the response to it are reconceived is perceived as colluding with evil. Terrorism is responded to with more terrorism. Flag waving is responded to with the waving of protest signs. Threats to normative sexual and gender arrangements are responded to with aggressive demonstrations of normativity. Or conversely, oppressive gender labeling systems are responded to with re-signifying practices that rely on the valorization of previously degrading labels ('queer') and the denigration of previously dominant signifiers ('hets' for heterosexuals) for their coherence. This latter move recalls Badiou's *simulacrum*. And how often in education courses for teachers is the evil construed in terms of the homophobes who torment the victim, a move Badiou would label *disaster*? How often the response to the posited *a priori* evil of sexism, homophobia or racism is framed in terms of valorizing a fixed cultural, racial, or sexual identity. Such a move, according to Badiou, would be terror. Why? Because, as Badiou writes, '[T]he enemy of a true subjective fidelity is precisely the closed set, the substance of the situation, the community ... . Every invocation of blood and soil, of race, of custom, of community works directly against truths' (Badiou, 2001, p. 76).

The third problem with positing evil as an *a priori* and ethics as a response to this evil is that we are prevented from thinking the singularity of situations as such. Evil is massified, and as a result the particularity of the situation is ignored, and the actual here-and–now response is cast in terms of a general response, which erases or diminishes the maximum possibility of responding to the singularity of the event. We have no way to understand how or why someone would choose to act as he or she does, because evil, rendered as something beyond us, is construed as simply infecting us or irrationally taking us over such that we need to return to a state prior to the emergence of such evil.

Thus, exploring why particular individuals who commit so-called terrorist acts or why specific individuals who beat up Arab-Americans or ostracize gay youth, do as they do, is foreclosed by the positing of an *a priori* evil in the form of terrorism, racism, heterosexism. The specificity of the situation is erased by the massified evil, however that evil is defined.

Ethics as a Response to the Other

The second way teachers and educators often frame pedagogical ethics is in terms of the Other, be that other foreign to oneself or an aspect of oneself. Here ethics concerns itself with ensuring that children and adolescents are tolerant and respectful of one another and of themselves. We see this ethics in the various mainstream approaches to multicultural education, and attempts to build self-esteem.

Certainly at face value there appears little wrong with an ethics of tolerance, an ethics that Michael Walzer (1997) describes in *On Toleration* as the work of democratic citizens. Following Badiou, I want to suggest, however, that an ethics based on respecting the Other, be that Other intra-psychic or external, must appeal to either metaphysics or must fall into an inconsistency. It is inconsistent because, without metaphysics, without positing the divine or God within each of us, not all differences are tolerated. For example, intolerance is not tolerated in such an ethics. The white supremacist is not tolerated or respected in such an ethics, nor is the militant Islamic fundamentalist, perhaps because both experience a *jouissance* unavailable to us. The racist enjoys unbridled expression of hatred that liberal society often masks. The militant Islamic fundamentalist embraces a faith unto death that many in the West romanticize.

An ethics of tolerance must resort to theology because as there is only difference, both within myself and between myself and others, either one treats all differences unequally, which contradicts the claim of tolerance, or one posits an absolute sameness in each person, for example the divine or God. Badiou writes, 'There are as many differences, say between a Chinese peasant and a young Norwegian professional as between myself and anybody at all, including myself' (Badiou, 2001, p. 26). To treat these differences equally is to respect some transcendent quality in each that totalizes the differences. I certainly follow Badiou's rejection of such a totalization and read it as leading to the very *disaster* that he sees as one of the faces of evil.

We can also see such an ethics of the Other expressed in the energy spent on ensuring students develop self-esteem and take pride in their gender, sexuality, race, ethnicity, and culture. The problem is that such self-esteem or pride can reify our identities, and foreclose an examination of the multitude within. As Badiou writes, 'Every appeal to community organizes an evil, including appeals to America or France' (Badiou, 2001, p. 86).

Ethics as Obedience to the Law

The third way that mainstream conceptions of the ethics of teaching are framed is in terms of obedience to the Law. Here ethics emerges as acting in accordance with moral, legal or natural dictates. Whether students are required to follow the rules developed by their own classmates or simply disciplined for not obeying the school rules, whether children and adolescents are urged or forced to conform to 'natural' ways of behaving or admonished to obey the law, ethical action is framed in terms of one's duty to obey. The obvious example here was the willingness of so many citizens to give up their rights because the government was asking them to, and their willingness to frame the Iraq war as a battle between morality and immorality, between the civilized world and the non-civilized world. The problem, of course, is that questioning or stepping outside such a frame casts one as unethical.

But the more interesting problem with framing pedagogical ethics in terms of obeying moral, legal or natural dictates concerns the dark side of such an ethics. Following Lacan here, rather than Badiou, I would argue that for the law, be it moral, natural or juridical, to exert compliance, it must appear just and fair in the light of day, but it must offer, to those who obey, the secret pleasure of knowing it is enforced through methods that must remain in the dark. As Žižek puts it, 'What holds a community most deeply is not so much identification with the Law that regulates the community's normal everyday circuit, but rather identification with a specific form of transgression of the Law, of the Law's suspension' (1994, p. 55). It is finally this violence that holds together the natural law that, for example, orders gender and sexuality. It is the unleashing of any means necessary, including torture and assassination, which provides a secret pleasure to those interested in protecting the laws of the US. One can see this dark side in operation in teachers' who take delight in failing or harassing students for the students' own good, and appeal to school rules and norms to justify their own meanness.

These then are the three approaches to pedagogical ethics dominant today. Badiou and Lacan help us problematize all three. How, though, does their work help us re-think a pedagogical ethics? What ethics of teaching might emerge from their theorization? In the next section, I offer what I call an alternative to mainstream ethics of teaching, one that is informed by both Badiou and Lacan.

The Ethics of Teaching

The pedagogical ethics I offer here provides a way to think about the encounter with terror, loss, anguish and confusion or with the Real, that is the 'traumatic, irreducible, essentially asocial and asymbolic particularity of [one's] experience' (Hallward, 2001, p. xvii). Such an ethics allows us to be present, when an event calls us, transforming us in the process. By 'present' I refer to a state that is open, attentive, and focused on the here-and-now, although not lost in the moment. Such an ethics does posit living truthfully as its animating principle, but attempts to make a place for the unconscious in its approach to truth. If, as the Dalai Lama says, all living beings have the right to freedom from suffering, it is equally true, as Freud pointed out, that many of us find excessive pleasure in suffering. Therefore in developing such an ethics we cannot avoid confronting the complexity of the unconscious and desire. Furthermore, I would argue such an ethics cannot require or aspire to the repudiation of the quotidian. Rather, it requires that we try to understand how our quotidian lives are not only conditioned, but also how they are shot through with unconscious desires and libidinal investments. It is not a question of shattering the quotidian and emerging contemporaneously as a new subject, committed to an evental truth-process. Rather, it is a question of living in the complexity of one's life and adhering to the truth of that complexity, a truth which involves assuming responsibility for the way one's desires and psychic investments conjure and inform that irreducible complexity. Let us take an example from teaching.

You are in a high school classroom, teaching. The day is hot, some kids are distracted. Others participate in a conversation about a poem. Quietly, you are thinking a million thoughts, trying to figure out what is happening with different kids, with your own feelings, with your life and with the poem. You are not lost in driving towards an objective, nor are you ahead of yourself running on automatic. You try as much as possible to be sensitive to all the little flurries, vibrations, looks, and feelings around you: a kid's sneakers are soiled and untied; your shirt is sweaty; boredom is creeping around the edges of the poem and your consciousness. Someone is laughing. Suddenly the door bangs open. A big kid rushes in, yelling that there is a strike about the war. Noise roars in from the hallway. Students are running or walking in the hallways. A protest? What's happening? It's about the war. Kids are protesting, leaving the building. You lose focus. A bunch of your students rush to the window. Shouts and excited clamoring of 'Can we leave?' as some students are already out the door. Something is happening. You are swept up. You are frightened. You are excited. You are not a teacher right now. Who are you? What do you want? You hate the war and the administration; its horrors are beyond your imagination. Letting in its horrors would be too much, but you always talk against the war. You've protested before. What do you do?

So let us stop here. For Badiou, such a scenario presents a situation opening up the possible irruption of an event whose truth could emerge through this teacher's commitment to it in perhaps joining with students pouring out of schools all over the city. The void now appears—teaching in a time of war. Students are naming the event. Perhaps this is it. Paris '68. New York '07. Such a teacher would be acting ethically, according to Badiou, by joining such a protest and remaining faithful to the consequences of 'No more business as usual!'. Certainly that would be a kind of fidelity to one's truth, if in fact that teacher took such an action. But what about the teacher who didn't leave? What of the teacher who remains inside the building, frightened, troubled, suspicious, perhaps resentful? Is such a teacher less ethical, less of an Immortal? And what of the school administrator, who, condoning the protests, nevertheless contemplates holding those students who walked out accountable? Is such an administrator unethical in Badiou's sense of an ethics?

My response to these questions is that the teacher who joins the protest, the teacher who lingers behind, and the administrator who follows regulations may or may not be ethical. What determines the ethicality of their choice is their willingness to assume responsibility for their libidinal investments in their choices. In other words, what determines or measures the ethical nature of their choice is their willingness to own their desires. What does that mean?

From a Lacanian perspective, ethics involves not giving ground on one's desire. This does not mean simply following one's desire, regardless of what it is, and assuming the consequences of such an act. It certainly does not mean following the imperative to Enjoy! or pursue the objects of desire. Such a move would catch us in the trap of the law and its transgression and keep us prisoner of the situation in Badiou's meaning of situation. Not to give ground on one's desire means to follow one's desire in order to understand its coordinates, how it is staged within fantasy, and, from a position that is bereft of secure identities or comfort in some transcendental Other, to take full responsibility for one's desire. So, let us return to the scenario I sketched above.

What would render the two teachers' and the administrator's various choices unethical would be, for example, if the first teacher disavowed his desire to be liked by the students, his own investments in the enthusiasm that grips him and the ego-ideal it provided, and how these contributed to his joining the protest. Or if the second teacher failed to acknowledge his belief in academics as separate from politics, saying he wanted to go but was staying behind to make sure the building was protected. Or if the administrator, denying his own anticipated pleasure in punishing some students, claimed he was just doing his duty.

The pedagogical ethics I am proposing here asks us to face our own desires, to risk our safety and notions of who we are, to explore our own complicity in what befalls us, and to take a hard look at our own histories, individual and collective. It asks that we do this without thoughtlessly donning the lenses of fixed identities and familiar egos or succumbing to the allure of seemingly neutral and reasonable normalizing discourses that impute to individuals, children or adults, a nature that is exempt from contingency and outside history. It asks us not to fall back on familiar even archaic identities and structures of feeling, when the lynch pins of our seemingly stable but actually provisional identities loosen or crumble, lynch pins such as the World Trade Towers or the Berlin Wall or the Name of the Father or heteronormativity or a seemingly happy marriage or a secure job. And it requires that we bracket an appeal to principle as the cause of our action and consider the other desires that suffuse those choices. The consideration of such desires and the willingness not to give up on them means that not only is the very attachment to identity, feelings, and principle surrendered but so is the collapse into desire itself. Such an ethics, of course, requires a psychoanalytic understanding[1] of our singular experience.

And this singular experience returns us to Badiou and Lacan. An ethics of presence requires a commitment to one's singular truth in the face of the Real, but the truth to which one commits is the truth of one's responsibility for the world one inhabits, the meanings one attaches to that world. However the teacher or administrator reacts to the student walkout, the truth-process emerges in the analysis of psychic investments and the openness to feel what is happening such that one can rigorously analyze those investments. Yes, an encounter with the Real shatters what was, just as an event breaks into, and if one can remain faithful to its truth-process, transfigures a situation, and yes, both open the way of ethical action, but unlike Badiou, I would argue that the fidelity to what emerges requires the willingness to sustain a psychoanalysis of one's desires, one's psychic investments in what is happening, not to become them but to follow them and thus in a sense give them up by not identifying with them but still remaining true to them. Let me offer here one final example, one that comes from Hollywood rather than the classroom.

At the end of *Casablanca*, the cynical Rick played by Humphrey Bogart is forced to make a choice and chooses to sacrifice the love of his life so she can accompany her husband whose immeasurable importance to the resistance would dissipate without her by his side. In parting, Rick reminds her that, compared to the political reality, their romantic problems are 'not worth a hill of beans'. Rick has re-joined the struggle against fascism. Rick's decision to ensure Ilsa's and her husband's escape constitutes his fidelity to the truth of an event that changes the situation and transforms him into an Immortal or a subject. It is a compelling story, but what is missing is any contemplation on Rick's part or any suggestion on the part of the storyteller of what psychic investments Rick may have had in making such a choice. It was those psychic investments that, we can retroactively say, constituted the story. After all, had Rick gone with Ilsa and left her husband to carry on or had he stayed with her husband and put Ilsa on the plane, each of those decisions could be justified by the plot (Žižek, 1992). What is important to understand is Rick's desire. It is not that he shouldn't have made the decision he did; it is that his fidelity should have also been to a process of examining his own libidinal investments in that choice. One might speculate that given his history, his real desire is to be always leaving: to leave New York, to leave the Spanish communists, to leave Paris. Even Ilsa's leaving him the first time can be read as his own desire realized, just as her leaving him at the end is an abandonment he, himself, engineers. The second time appears to be a more consciously engineered departure, but his claim that it is in the name of a greater good can be interpreted as a rationalization of his compulsion to leave. Such a rationalization constitutes, for Lacan, a faux ethical act. As Alenka Zupančič argues, 'Lacan ... formulates the question of ethics in terms of ... a "choice that is motivated by no good"' (Zupančič, 1998, p. 109). Or, as Slavoj Žižek (2007) argues, Rick's decision can be interpreted as a 'cruel narcissistic act of vengeance ... a punishment for [Ilsa's] letting him down in Paris' (p. 143). Or, just to turn the screw another notch, does not Rick's sacrifice perhaps conceal his own desire to sustain the belief that the paternal figure, Ilsa's heroic husband, is not flawed? The big Other is kept whole, ensuring Rick's heroic position in the scheme of things or what Lacan called the Symbolic. Of course, these are speculations. My aim in making them is to suggest that the ethical act involves a willingness to engage in a radical analysis of one's desire such that one risks one's ontological moorings, one's identity, even the fantasmatic kernel of who one is and has been.

While it sounds heroic to claim a new subjecthood and immortality, in Badiou's sense, through fidelity to a truth-process, I believe it is harder and perhaps more ethical to stay open to the psychic complexity of whatever the situation might entail, and to risk exploring one's psychic investments in the event that will have become that to which one commits oneself, whether that is to walk out of the school in the protest, remain in the school, hold the students accountable, or in the case of *Casablanca*, to sacrifice one's love. It is the exploration of one's psychic investments and one's desires, the willingness to keep open the question of one's choice while making a choice that constitutes a pedagogical ethics.

Our unconscious, our psychic life underlies and shoots through the self that is mired in the day-to-day, all too familiar routines of our lives. Only by remaining open to that self as well to exploring it psychoanalytically might we resist the lure of collapsing into the perhaps selfless, but I would argue, blind 'Immortal'. Badiou writes, 'self-interest is anti-thetical to the truth process' (2001, p. 60). I believe it is that very self-interest that must be explored, understood as an overdetermined attachment and a defense against change but also as an opening that allows for a counter-balance against the totalization of the new. 'The Immortal exists only in and by the mortal animal ... the world as world is and will remain between the true and the false' (Badiou, 2001, pp. 84–85). While it is compelling to imagine ourselves seized by an event and remaining faithful to its truth-process, it is equally important to follow our desires and acknowledge our psychic investments. Renouncing or waffling on the rigor of analysis constitutes a betrayal of ourselves, for we then become blind to our involvement in our reality, and risk succumbing to what Badiou labels the maxim of opinion which is: ' "Love only that which you have always believed" ' (2001, p. 52).

We have established that an ethics of teaching emerges at the moment of confrontation with the Real, and that such an encounter occurs by chance: one never knows in advance when one will be confronted by the Real or be seized by an event. One can only remain open or present to such a possibility. Furthermore, following Badiou, I have argued that commitment to the truth of the event, a commitment, not stripped of self-interest but aware of its own self-interest as defined by utilitarian goods, is integral to such an ethics. Such awareness requires a sustained self-examination, one I would argue that occurs through an interminable psychoanalysis. One must persist in that commitment without rendering it a good for all. The Good must 'not aspire to render the world good' (Badiou, 2001, p. 85). Therefore, 'it must be that the power of a truth is also a kind of powerlessness', because '[e]very absolutization of the power of truth organizes an Evil' (Badiou, 2001, p. 85). And is not a central tenet of Lacan's psychoanalytic theory that we must accept our own fundamental castration or powerlessness while we continue to act in the world?

But if we are to live with that powerlessness, if that powerlessness, as Badiou and Lacan understand it, is necessary to keep us from evil, then we must continually question and analyze our own desire. Such questioning and analysis allows that 'the space of the possible is larger than the one we are assigned—that something else is possible but not everything is possible' (Badiou, 2001, p. 86). Not everything is possible, and yet, in the space of a moment, if one commits to one's truth, be it the truth of one's desires and the truth of one's choice, if one does not betray that truth, or impose it, or collapse into it, and if one can live in that moment without safety, a new world opens, and an old one comes to an end.

Note

1. It is beyond the scope of this chapter to elaborate the specifics of the psychoanalytic approach I am advocating. I have detailed these specifics elsewhere (Taubman, 1999, 2000, 2001, 2002, 2006, 2007).

References

Badiou, A. (2001) *Ethics: An essay on the understanding of evil*, P. Hallward, trans. (New York, Verso Press).

Baldwin, J. (1985) *The Price of the Ticket: Collected Nonfiction 1948–1985* (New York, St. Martin's Press).

Baldwin, J. (1987) Interview conducted by Peter Taubman, March 10 (telephone interview with James Baldwin).

Hallward, P. (2001) Translator's Introduction, in: A. Badiou (ed.), *Ethics: An essay on the understanding of evil*, P. Hallward, trans. (New York, Verso Press), pp. vii–xlvii.

Hersh, S. (2005) Seymour Hersh: Iraq 'Moving Towards Open Civil War', interview with Amy Goodman, *Democracy Now: The War and Peace Report*, available at http://www.democracynow.org/2005/5/11/seymour_hersh_iraq_moving_towards_open.

Kesson, K. (2007) Philosophy or Philosophemes: Developing an ethics of curriculum work. Presented at the Eighth Annual Curriculum and Pedagogy Conference, Marble Falls, Texas.

Kuhn, T. S. (1962) *The Structure of Scientific Revolutions* (Chicago, University of Chicago Press).

Lacan, J. (1988) *The Seminar of Jacques Lacan: Book I Freud's papers on technique 1953–1954*, J. Miller, ed.; D. Porter, trans. (New York, W.W. Norton & Co.).

Lacan, J. (1992) *The Seminar of Jacques Lacan: Book VII The ethics of psychoanalysis 1959–1960*, J. Miller, ed.; J. Forreter, trans. (New York, W.W. Norton & Co.).

Ragland, E. (1996) An Overview of the Real, with Examples from Seminar I, in: R. Feldstein, B. Fink & M. Januus (eds), *Reading Seminar I and II: Lacan's return to Freud* (New York, SUNY Press).

Sartre, J-P. (1947) *Existentialism* (New York, The Philosophical Library, Inc.).

Taubman, P. (1999) Silent Voices, Talking Cures: Pedagogy as therapy, pedagogy as analysis, *JCT: The Journal of Curriculum Theorizing*, 15:2, pp. 3–15.

Taubman, P. (2000) Teaching without Hope: What Is Really at Stake in the Standards Movement, High Stakes Testing, and the Drive for Practical Reforms, *JCT: The Journal of Curriculum Theorizing*, 16:3, pp. 5–20.

Taubman, P. (2001) 'The Callings of Sexual Identities', in: G. Hudak & P. Kihn (eds), *Labeling: Politics and pedagogy* (London, The Falmer Press), pp. 179–199.

Taubman, P. (2002) Facing the Terror Within: Exploring the personal in multicultural education, in: C. Korn & A. Bursztyn (eds), *Case Studies in Cultural Transitions: Rethinking multicultural education* (Chicago, Greenwood Press), pp. 97–129.

Taubman, P. (2006) I Love Them to Death, in: G. Boldt & P. Salvio (eds), *On the Return of Love and Childhood: Psychoanalytic theory in teaching and learning* (New York, Routledge Press), pp. 19–32.

Taubman, P. (2007) The Beautiful Soul of Teaching: The contribution of psychoanalytic thought to critical self reflection and reflective practice, in: M. Gordon & T. O'Brien (eds), *Bridging the Gap between Theory and Practice* (Rotterdam, Sense Publishers), pp. 1–17.

Tobin, J. (ed.) (1997) *Making a Place for Pleasure in Early Childhood Education* (New Haven, CT, Yale University Press).

Walzer, M. (1997) *On Toleration: the Castle Lectures on ethics, politics and economic* (New Haven, CT, Yale University Press).

Žižek, S. (1992) *Looking Awry: An Introduction to Jacques Lacan through popular culture* (Boston, MIT Press).

Žižek, S. (1994) *The Metastases of Enjoyment: Six essays on woman and causality* (New York, Verso Press).

Žižek, S. (2007) *The indivisible remainder: on Schelling and related matters* (New York, Verso Press).

Zupančič, A. (1998) Lacan's Heroines: Antingone and Sygne de Coufontaine, *New Formations: A Journal of Culture/Theory/Politics*, 35:Autumn, pp. 108–121.

5

Reconceptualizing Professional Development for Curriculum Leadership: Inspired by John Dewey and informed by Alain Badiou

KATHLEEN R. KESSON & JAMES G. HENDERSON

> If dogmas and institutions tremble when a new idea appears, this shiver is nothing to what would happen if the idea were armed with the means for the continuous discovery of new truth and the criticism of old belief. (John Dewey, 1999/1929, p. 76)

> I shall call 'truth' (*a* truth) the real process of a fidelity to an event: that which this fidelity *produces* in the situation. (Alain Badiou, 2001, p. 42)

In our first opening quotation, Dewey alludes to the intransigence of institutions, be they social institutions or institutions of thought, and he celebrates the power of new ideas, informed by insightful critique and continuous inquiry, to challenge ideological and institutional 'regimes of truth'. In our second opening quotation, Badiou posits 'truth' as the product of an existential process—the expression of an inspired, transformative awakening in a particular situation. Badiou writes that all human situations are complex, open-ended phenomena that recede into infinity. Hence, no one can claim that they have acquired a transcendent overview of any particular situation. However, individuals can experience an event in a particular situation that inspires them to speak a truth 'for all'. Such a truth is 'democratic' in that it includes all humanity and, perhaps, all species on the planet (Badiou, 2005a). This truth inspiration, which endures after the specific event has occurred, 'compels the subject to *invent* a new way of being and acting in the situation' (pp. 41–2). We perceive an important connection between Badiou's 'invention of new ways of being and acting in particular situations' and Dewey's call for a 'continuous discovery of new truth'; furthermore, we believe that there are some clues here to how educators and curriculum leaders might develop forms of intelligent action capable of deposing the technical/ managerial, or 'standardized management' paradigm, that has for so long structured their work and limited the possibilities for democratic education.

We begin with a number of premises that constitute the groundwork for our proposal for reconceptualizing the professional development of educators. First, we believe that education in the United States should be oriented towards the historic problem of preparing citizens for life in a democratic society. Second, our conception of democratic life includes but exceeds political life; in this, we adhere to both Dewey's (1939/1989) position that 'democracy is a way of life ... which provides a moral standard for personal conduct' (p. 101) and more recently Judith Green's (1999) notion of 'deep' democracy as a way of life characterized by empathy, equity, commitment, and connection. Third, we characterize the present moment as a multifaceted 'crisis in democracy' exacerbated and accelerated by such events as the recent economic chaos, the domestic and international 'war on terror', the potential ecological catastrophe in the form of climate change, and other pressing biosphere concerns. Fourth, we believe that the professional training of most educators falls short of preparing them with the knowledge, dispositions, and capacities to both understand the depth of the crises and to respond to the challenges with 'ethical fidelity'—a concept from Badiou (2001) that will be elaborated in this chapter. We propose here a rethinking of the framework for the professional development of educators across the career life span that is inspired by Dewey's challenge to educate for democratic living. We amplify, elaborate and attempt to refine Dewey's challenge with the more contemporary thinking of Alain Badiou, who helps us understand the important relationships between truth as inspirational awakening, subjectification as existential commitment, and ethical fidelity as 'for all' action.

Introducing a Reconceptualized Professional Development

We want to contextualize our professional development proposal in what Badiou, following Sartre, names a *situation*—literally, the givens in which we find ourselves: our language, our heritage, the cultural milieu, our personal histories, the current state of politics (or politics of the State), etc.—what philosophers call our 'facticity'. This section gives a brief description of the current 'situation' that educational workers inhabit and a brief overview of how professional development is generally conceived in our current historical situation. We then note what we believe are the limitations of mainstream thinking on this vital educational topic, and explore how the work of both Dewey and Badiou might support a framework and practical strategies that would strengthen educators' commitments to educating for deep democracy, despite enormous contemporary challenges.

We reiterate that most educational practice in US public schools functions within what we call the 'standardized management paradigm' with its focus on the problem of test performances and its solution of scripted or prescribed curriculum and instruction enforced by state accountability mandates. This hierarchical organization of labor, with its concomitant deskilling of teachers (Apple, 1988), is mitigated only slightly by the competing 'constructivist best practice paradigm' with its focus on the problem of performances of subject matter understanding informed by traditions of disciplined/disciplinary knowing. Professional development, which begins at the pre-service level and continues throughout teachers' careers, generally falls within the overlapping and tension-filled parameters of these two paradigms of practice. As in other professions (medical, legal, etc.), continuing education is necessary to stay abreast of current 'best practices' in one's chosen field.

Professional development opportunities are many and varied: they may look like the classic 'in-service' day, with outside experts brought in for one-shot infusions of new ideas (differentiated curriculum, diversity, assertive discipline, technology integration), or they might focus on 'product implementation' (Hinchey & Cadiero-Kaplan, 2005)—training by consultants whose services are tied to the corporate-created curricula that many teachers are now required to implement in their classrooms. Staff development of teachers is more often like a fast-food cafeteria than a satisfying full course meal: offerings might include isolated curriculum initiatives, the latest teaching fad, or increasingly, how to interpret test scores and teach to the test. Many initiatives are fragmented, top-down, and embody, according to Fullan and Hargreaves, 'a passive view of the teacher, who is empty, deficient, lacking in skills, needing to be filled up and fixed with new techniques and strategies' (1996, p. 17).

Increasingly, professional development has been linked to both student achievement and school reform; and at least at the level of influential professional and governmental organizations such as the American Educational Research Association (see Resnick, 2005) and the Federal Department of Education (http://www.ed.gov/pubs/AchGoal4/mission.html), there is growing recognition that professional development needs to be more systemic, and focus on both the subject matter that teachers will be teaching and on how students learn particular subject matter (pedagogical content knowledge). To this end, prescriptions for professional development across the mainstream liberal/reform movement include many of the following aims:

- Acquisition of more in-depth content knowledge,
- Learning how to set and achieve high academic standards,
- Development of curriculum units with more sophisticated content that can be implemented in classrooms,
- Learning new instructional methods to teach challenging content,
- Developing capacity to teach to a variety of learning styles and differentiate instruction,
- Gaining familiarity with 'data' and how to read these so as to increase student achievement,
- Creating learning communities for discussion and reflection with colleagues about best practices

In this chapter, we start from the premise that even 'holistic' prescriptions for teacher development, which include all or part of this spectrum of aims, which take into account teacher beliefs and knowledge, the cultural context of the school, and differing teachers' needs, and which avoid faddism and foster collaboration and shared learning, are necessary but not sufficient to the contemporary challenges of teaching in a democratic society, or more to the point, a society with democratic aspirations. Such prescriptions, taken as a whole, represent the 'constructivist best practices' paradigm, which to some extent transcends the standardized management paradigm (see Henderson & Gornik, 2007) but fails to meet the challenging standard of democratic educational practice. Such prescriptions also fail to resolve the inescapable contradictions in the contemporary labor conditions of teaching 'professionals': educators' decisions are considered, chosen, and carried out in a bureaucratic context in which rules and procedures govern most action and in which there is little opportunity to exercise ethical volition. This work context is characterized by top-down policy making and rigid supervision hierarchies, a discourse of accountability focused on a narrow, testable range of outcomes, and increasingly punitive measures for non-compliance with standardized and bureaucratic rules. Thus, teachers have little opportunity to exercise 'constructivist best practices' when these conflict with bureaucratic imperatives.

We find the liberal/reform professional development recommendations in the constructivist best practices paradigm to be accommodative and ameliorative at best, rather than transformative; in general, they encourage teachers to improve what they are doing so as to better attain the goals set for them by bureaucratic 'experts', rather than to challenge the underlying assumptions of their work and their work environments. In simple curriculum studies terms, they are concerned with the 'hows', not the 'whys', of teaching. While we would not argue with any of the general goals listed above (although many debates should rightly occur concerning the specifics of these propositions), we want to suggest that they are insufficient for understanding the complex, multidimensional nature of 'democratic' experience (Green, 1999; Jay, 2005), and further, that the current crises of democracy (Henderson & Kesson, 2004) present a specific historical challenge to educators. We propose an orientation to this challenge that might open us to ways of being, knowing, and doing congruent with deep democracy (Green, 1999). A reconceptualized professional development standard might be stated thusly: *Teachers who hope to facilitate 'deep' subject matter understanding integrated with democratic self and social learning ('3S' learning) with their students must develop a sophisticated understanding of the nature, function, dynamics, and possibilities of deep democracy as well as its challenges.* A second reconceptualized standard might read thusly: *Educators in democratic societies will explore their most deeply held values and commitments and develop strategies for teaching in a manner that is congruent with these.*

Our premise is that the dominant standardized management paradigm is inconsistent with deep democracy and that the constructivist best practices paradigm, while not inconsistent, is inadequate. If teachers hope to break free of the standardized management paradigm, a radical 'rupture' of the magnitude of an 'event' (Badiou, 2001) is necessary. To this end, we propose a disciplined approach to professional development that requires a contemplative (currere/self-knowledge) stance, is grounded in a curriculum studies-based/complicated conversation approach to inquiry, and culminates in a theoretically informed approach to deliberation and decision-making that is oriented towards facilitating a balanced '**3S**' education (again, referring to 'deep' subject matter understanding integrated with democratic self and social learning.) The intent here is to position curriculum and teaching as a *democratic wisdom challenge*.

Inspired by John Dewey

We propose a *differentiated* and *disciplined* approach to professional development that is designed to support a particular kind of continuing education across a democratic teacher's career. We use the qualifier, *differentiated* professional development in two specific ways. Our audience is educators who experience a vocational calling to embody and enact democracy-in-education and are, therefore, inclined to question, challenge and establish critical distance from mainstream professional development. The educators we have in mind view themselves as 'artists' and want to be treated accordingly. By making a distinction between education as applied science and inspired artistry, they would resonate with Dewey's (1897/2004) articulation of his pedagogical beliefs:

> Education ... is a process of living and not a preparation for future living ... . Much of present education fails because it neglects this fundamental principle of the school as a form of [democratic] community life ... . Education thus conceived marks the most perfect and intimate union of science and art conceivable in human experience. The art of thus giving shape to human powers and adapting them to social service is the supreme art; one calling into its service the best of artists; that no insight, sympathy, tact, executive power, is too great for such a service. Every teacher should realize the dignity of his [or her] calling ... . (pp. 18–19, 23)

Since artists are, by definition, committed to the idiosyncrasies of their own unique 'callings', the educators we have in mind are also comfortable with a personally *differentiated* professional development. They would resonate with Eisner's (1994) notion of 'productive idiosyncrasy', aptly summarized by Uhrmacher and Matthews (2005):

> During an era obsessed with issues of conformity and standardization, Eisner follows a different path. Influenced by the work of Sir Herbert Read, Eisner argues that education should foster *productive idiosyncrasy* among students, rather than mold all to standard uniformity. In short, he is interested in helping children learn to use their senses to achieve greater degrees of perceptive and expressive differentiation, so that they may formulate concepts and represent them through a variety of forms. (p. 6, authors' emphasis)

We use the qualifier, *disciplined* professional development, to refer to the discipline-from-within that accompanies a vocational calling for democratic education. Our sense of discipline-from-within is informed by van Manen's (1991) discussion of 'pedagogical intent' and Kreisberg's (1992) analysis of 'power-with' relations in education. Standing in contrast to this understanding of the use of 'power' would be the various power-over practices with their hierarchical structures and strategies, as examined by Foucault (1980) and many other 'postmodern' critical theorists. Also standing in contrast to our understanding of discipline-from-within are the various structural interpretations of the academic disciplines, perhaps most significantly the 'structures-of-disciplines' movement in curriculum studies during the late 1950s and early 1960s (Ford & Pugno, 1964).

As advocates of an internal 'disciplinarity' (Pinar, 2007), we encourage, nurture, honor and applaud diversified 'lines of flight' (Deleuze & Guattari, 1980/1987) as concrete expressions of productive idiosyncrasy. We invite and affirm multiple interpretive trajectories, as long as they are expressions of a discipline-from-within. Inspired by Greene's (1988) sense of personal-public freedom, we acknowledge the plurality of voices associated with authentic quests. In the spirit of democratic living—that is, *power of, by, for the people*, as evoked by Dewey (1938/1998): 'to paraphrase the saying of Lincoln about democracy, one of education of, by, and for experience' (p. 19), we summarily reject all attempts to homogenize and stand-ardize human understanding and expression, and we recognize that such attempts are grounded in an authoritarian logic. In sum, the notion of *disciplined openness* is central to our conception of professional development.

Three Forms of Disciplinary Artistry

Our differentiated and disciplined approach to professional development is guided by forms of disciplinary artistry that are based on three interpretations of Pinar's (2007) concept of curriculum 'disciplinarity'. Pinar's geometric visual model includes a *vertical* dimension, referring to 'the intellectual history of the discipline' (Pinar, 2007, p. xiii) and a *horizontal* dimension, referring to 'analyses of ... [and experience with] the field's present set of intellectual circumstances ... [including] the social and political milieus which influence and, all too often, structure this set (Pinar, 2007, p. xiv). As Pinar (2007) elaborates, 'verticality documents the ideas that constitute curriculum studies' (p. xiv), while horizontality acknowledges the importance of here-and-now deliberative artistry. We have added to Pinar's model the idea of a *diagonal* dimension (which is implicit but not explicit in his model), referring to the dynamic personal understandings and broadening of 'horizons' (Gadamer, 1975) generated at the vertical-horizontal interface through processes of 'currere compositions' (Pinar, 2004). With this elaboration of Pinar's useful model, we affirm the personal journey (at once intellectual, practical, and activist) that we believe is essential to developing a 'love of democratic wisdom' (Henderson & Kesson, 2004).

Applying the vertical dimension to our professional development approach fore-grounds an **inquiry artistry** exemplified by a particular scholarly 'arc' in John Dewey's career: the movement from articulating a platform of pedagogical beliefs with reference to democracy and education, to conceptualizing thoughtful practice and community, to undertaking democratic educational practices, to engaging in diversified studies of 'educative experience', to considering 'culture' as the proper focus for this study. This key arc in Dewey's scholarly career provides a vivid illus-tration of disciplined inquiry guided by an open set of inquiries (epistemological, ethical, aesthetic, political). In effect, Dewey practices a highly diversified inquiry that is informed by a 'love of wisdom' and that is directed toward the democrati-zation of educational experience (Garrison, 1997). Applying the horizontal dimen-sion to our professional development approach foregrounds a **deliberative artistry** informed by Schwab's (1969) 'arts of the practical' and 'arts of the eclectic' and given concrete form in Henderson and Gornik's *Transformative Curriculum Leadership* (2008). Applying the diagonal dimension to our professional development approach foregrounds a **contemplative artistry** informed by Pinar's (2004) 'currere' self-examination and Nash's (2004) scholarly personal narratives.

Diagonality represents the journey of a courageous and experimental educator, with a mindset capable of embracing paradox, rupture, and uncertainty (Deleuze, 1994), as well as an inclination toward the critical self-examination that lies at the heart of democratic ethical fidelity in education (Badiou, 2001). However, the notion of 'self-examination' as commonly understood in education takes on a different, more nuanced cast in Badiou's work. For Badiou, 'ethical fidelity' is not a process by which a stable subject (a 'self') pursues a fixed aim; rather, it refers to the way in which a 'becoming subject' is caught up in something larger than him or herself, carried away on the wave of an emerging truth. In this sense, an educator may be immersed in the situation generated at the interface of the vertical and the horizontal axes of study (the *givens* of a situation), but they also extend *beyond*; their ethical fidelity is literally a bridge between what is known and what is not known. Hence, diagonality, for us, with its 'in the world but not of it' stance, opens the possibilities for highly recursive ('folded') lines of flight (Deleuze, 1993; Deleuze & Guattari, 1980/1987 capable of dissolving the 'inherited and policed subjectivities' (Fleming, 2002, p. 10) imposed by the dominant hierarchies and organizational forms of the standardized management paradigm.

To state this in more straightforward terms, each educator who hopes to meet the democratic wisdom challenge must commit to a life of disciplined inquiry into the rich literature of the curriculum studies tradition, they must ground this study in the concrete realities of their professional lives, and they must develop the critical self-awareness, social commitment, and 'faith' (conceived broadly/secularly) that will enable them to resist bureaucratic mandates that do not serve deeply democratic interests as defined by themselves, their students, and their communities. We recognize that 'democratic interests' vary, are plural and multiple, are contested, and do not lend themselves to expert (outside) definition. Thus, individuals and communities must engage in pragmatic processes of democratic 'becoming', and we believe these processes are well served by the three forms of disciplinary artistry (inquiry, deliberation, and contemplation) outlined here.

Three Phases

We move now from the conceptual to the concrete. Our professional development approach is geared to the professional artistry associated with a particular interpretation of democratic educational practice, called transformative curriculum leadership, or TCL for short (Henderson & Gornik, 2007). TCL practices have six interrelated components:

- *reconceptualizing* educational standards (rethinking the nature of 'subject matter' with reference to the democratization of educational experiences (Dewey, 1938/1998),
- *undertaking* the necessary multi-modal reflective inquiries,
- *enacting* systemic deliberations with reference to the interplay between designing, planning, teaching, evaluating and organizing decisions,

- *building* disciplined stakeholder and disciplined professional learning communities,
- *exercising* 'public intellectual leadership' through creative efforts to inspire and inform the public imaginary),
- *composing* curriculum-as-currere narratives.

Note the ways in which these six TCL components represent various potential junctures along the vertical/horizontal/diagonal axes of curriculum disciplinarity. In our work with cohorts of curriculum leaders who are working on cultivating these components of their TCL work in schools, we have noted at least three overlapping, though not necessarily linear phases in understanding and practicing: an *emerging* phase, where the focus is on acquiring a basic working knowledge, and appreciation for, the complete TCL multi-component gestalt; an *engaging* phase, where the focus is on daily cultivating the necessary deliberative, inquiry and contemplative artistry; and a *generating* phase, where the focus is on initiating TCL projects that will, over time, involve all six components of the practice. In the emerging phase, educators reflect on such matters as enhanced student learning, practical feasibility, personal ambivalence, vocational calling, professional support, local community acceptance, and so on. Do they really want to become committed to this type of professional artistry? Educators move into the engaging phase as they become committed to the cultivation of the deliberative, inquiry and contemplative artistry and willingly initiate and actively participate in a *disciplined* professional learning community advancing this challenging professional standard. Educators move into the generating phase by identifying 'wiggle room' (Cuban, 2003) for TCL projects, creating appropriate leadership plans, and initiating these plans. Since most educational settings today are dominated by standardized instructional management with, perhaps, a slight nod to 'constructivist' practices, leverage points for this curriculum leadership need to be thoughtfully identified and carefully addressed.

We conceptualize these phases as key turning points in a transformative curriculum leader's professional development; and though the phases should not be viewed as distinctive hierarchical stages, they are linked through a general developmental logic: from exploratory emergence to disciplinary engagement to assertive leadership. It is entirely possible that educators could collaboratively generate a TCL practice with only an emerging understanding of what is involved in this undertaking, and only over time begin to make a commitment to the required disciplined artistry.

Greene's (1988) discussion of 'spaces' of authentic engagement provides insight into our notion of overlapping phases. She writes:

> Looking back, we can discern individuals in their we-relations with others, inserting themselves in the world by means of projects, embarking on new beginnings in spaces they open themselves. We can recall them ... opening spaces where freedom is the mainspring, where people create themselves by acting in concert. (p. 134)

Applying Greene's notion of 'space', we can explain our three phases as follows. In an emerging space, the project is to acquire a basic understanding of the TCL gestalt; in an engaging space, the project is to undertake the necessary disciplined artistry; and in a generating space, the project is to initiate and sustain a TCL effort. It is entirely possible that particular educators could be authentically positioned within two or, even, three of these distinctive frames of reference.

We believe that good curriculum work is context- and case-specific and that the democracy and education relationship could be productively approached through 'arts' of understanding as informed by the tradition of philosophical hermeneutics, particularly the work of Gadamer (1975). Our first premise is informed by Schwab's (1969) 'arts of the practical', while the second is informed by Schwab's (1969) 'arts of the eclectic'. In effect, we take the position that there is a vital relationship between practicing *judgments* grounded in deliberative artistry and enacting *journeys* of understanding grounded in letter-of-the-word/spirit-of-the-matter interplay (Henderson & Gornik, 2007).

Through John Dewey's work, particularly his *Experience and Education* (1938/1998), we recognize the importance of rethinking democratic ideals in the 'here-and-now' of human experience. Such rethinking requires a 'heterodox' (Jay, 2005) approach to inquiry consistent with Pinar's (2004) argument that curriculum understanding is cultivated through 'complicated conversation'. Jackson's (2002) examination of Dewey's ambivalence concerning the substitution of 'culture' for 'experience', points to the culture-building consequences associated with the democratization of experience.[1] Finally, inspired by Dewey's (1929/1999) *Individualism Old and New*, we are intrigued by the challenges of personal 'becoming' that are embedded in the here-and-now of democratic 'being' (Aoki, 2005). We turn now to Badiou, whose ideas both illuminate and complicate commonsense understandings that we have inherited about the nature of the self, truth, democracy, and the process of transformation.

Informed by Alain Badiou

Our approach to professional development is informed by Alain Badiou's philosophical project. In his 'Preface to the English Edition', Badiou (2001) provides precise definitions of his ontological concepts: 'situation' and 'event'. He writes that, 'a situation must be conceived as both, in its *being,* a pure multiple ... and, in its *appearing,* as the effect of a transcendental legislation' (p. lvi) and that, 'an event is implicative, in the sense that it enables the detachment of a statement which will subsist as such once the event itself has disappeared' (pp. lvi–lvii, author's emphasis). Based on these ontological definitions, he then argues that an event in a situation 'compels the subject to *invent* a new way of being and acting in the situation' (pp. 41–42). He elaborates:

> Essentially, a truth is the material course traced, within the situation, by the evental supplementation. It is thus an *immanent break.* 'Immanent' because a truth proceeds *in* the situation, and nowhere else—there is no heaven of truths ... . I call 'subject' the bearer ... of a fidelity, the one who bears a process of truth. The subject, therefore, in no way pre-exists the process. He [or she] is absolutely nonexistent in the situation 'before' the

event. We might say that the process of truth *induces* a subject. (pp. 42–3, author's emphasis)

An *event*, for Badiou, is a 'happening which escapes all structuring "normality"' (2001, p. xvii), a rupture or break which presents the occasion for action through which the transformation of a *situation* might occur. A genuine event brings with it the conditions and the possibility for the emergence of a *truth*. When one becomes caught up in an event, there is a loss of self—the small, ego-centered self is literally taken over by something larger than the self. We become depersonalized 'subjects', bearers of a truth process. This truth process is akin to a paradigm shift (Kuhn, 1962); it reflects a theory of transformation that illuminates how the ordinary and the habitual might be superseded by *something else*—a something which was absent in the prior situation, or existed as potential in what Badiou calls the *void*: 'A truth punches a "hole" in knowledges, it is heterogeneous to them, but it is also the sole known source of new knowledges' (2001, p. 70). It is through *fidelity* to this emergence of a truth process that we live out an ethic of (a) truth. Fidelity 'amounts to a sustained investigation of the situation, under the imperative of the event itself; it is an immanent and continuing break' (ibid., p. 67). Badiou speaks of the courage and persistence required of this fidelity: 'Do all that you can to persevere in that which exceeds your perseverance. Persevere in the interruption. Seize in your being that which has seized and broken you' (ibid., p. 47).

We find that Badiou's ethical argument deeply informs our professional development approach, particularly with reference to Dewey's (1939/1989) position that 'democracy is a way of life … which provides a moral standard for personal conduct' (p. 101). We applaud Badiou's astute distancing from all forms of dogmatism. Obviously, dogmatism and democracy don't mix, and this is why we are enthusiastic advocates for the dialogical 'play' in Gadamer's (1975) hermeneutics. Such playfulness is a wonderful antidote for all forms of ideological scripting. In fact, we view rigid ideological consciousness, whether it be religious, political, intellectual, social or economic, as a cause for much of the human 'sickness' on the planet—what Badiou (2001) refers to as 'le Mal' (evil).

There is a humility embedded in Badiou's ethics that is quite consistent with the three dimensions of curriculum disciplinarity that we have introduced. Badiou (1988/2005a) situates his ethics at the edge of the 'void'—at the edge of an 'I don't know' that recedes into infinity. For Badiou, every 'situation' is constituted by an infinite set of elements, and humans must learn to be comfortable with complexity and mystery. In effect, from an ontological point of view, they have no choice. Certainly, humans must construct/make meaning to live purposeful lives, but it is important that they recognize that, often, what they consider to be 'solid' is actually an 'appearance' (Badiou, 2006) that is, always already, leaking into infinity (Badiou, 2005b). Such is human fate. We cannot be wise; we can only engage in a disciplined love of wisdom.

We acknowledge and affirm the pluralistic 'subjectification' processes at the heart of Badiou's ethics. No one gets to play 'God'; and in the context of a play of 'ethics of truth', anyone can speak 'for all' as long as they are persevering in their perspective without succumbing to *betrayal, delusion* and/or *terror*. These triple dangers speak to the many forms of human weakness that can manifest when people believe that they are guided by 'capital T' Truth—the multiple ways we have discovered to fall away from the good, the right, and the true. These include the many 'isms' that exclude and separate (ethnocentrism, geocentrism, racism, nativism, ableism, sexism and heterosexism, etc.); the temptation to betray one's personal ethics for personal gain or out of fear; or the tendency to think of one's truth as anything other than partial, contingent, and subject to change. We think that the result of such disciplined, mindful, existential subjectifications, if it was ever to occur beyond Socrates, Confucius, Buddha, Rabbi Hillel, Laozi and other historically significant 'teachers' (Armstrong, 2006), would be the realization of a cultural renaissance embedded in a Deweyan 'new' individualism.

This strikes us as a very worthy educational goal. In effect, we can imagine classrooms where teachers encourage the actualization of generative and generous student voices in the context of constructivist lessons. We have in mind students learning *curricular* 'subject matter' (Deng, 2007) that fosters Eisner's 'productive idiosyncrasy' (Uhrmacher & Matthews, 2005). Badiou's (2001) ethics allows for anyone to be 'convoked [*requis*] to be the immortal that he was not yet' (p. 40). We applaud his sense of universality, inclusivity, and fair play. Furthermore, we recognize the vital importance of ethical perseverance in education. Without educators who can sustain their 'for all' ethics over a long period of time, there doesn't seem to be much hope for the future of democracy in education. Are today's educators being prepared to be 'marathon runners', or are they only becoming constructivist best practice 'sprinters?' What kinds of changes might we see in education's purposes and practices if educators were challenged to be concerned about the long-term ethical consequences of their work?

Finally, we celebrate the inspirational subtext in Badiou's ethics. Democracy is more promise than reality. Democratic living requires visionary, courageous individuals who embody President Barak Obama's 'Yes We Can' motto and disposition. There have always been individuals who are willing to stand out from the crowd—from their current 'situation'—and speak democratic truth to power. We admire such individuals, and we are inspired by the educators that we have met who are willing to take on the challenges of enacting and embodying 'a love of democratic wisdom' in education (Garrison, 1997; Henderson & Kesson, 2004). Such educators have a calling that is inspired by specific personal and/or social 'events', and Badiou's ethics affirm this 'evental' phenomenology. Rosemary Gornik's currere narratives (in Henderson & Gornik, 2007) are powerful illustrations of this phenomenology. After sharing several personal events that have inspired her to persevere as a transformative curriculum leader, she concludes with this statement:

> Hopefully, you now have a better understanding of the educational road to a democratic 'good' life. By facilitating your journey of understanding, you are in a better position to encourage and support the journey of others, particularly students. By working in this way, you are contributing to the democratic future of our world. (p. 258)

From Montage Method to Portfolio Expression

Recall our early citation on Dewey's use of 'art' as a metaphor for education: 'The art of thus giving shape to human powers and adapting them to social service is the supreme art; one calling into its service the best of artists; that no insight, sympathy, tact, executive power, is too great for such a service'. It is no small task to come up with a method of professional development that avoids methodological dogma and is true to the notion of educational artistry, yet holds educators to rigorous practical and intellectual standards. We are faced with yet another dilemma in that we want to affirm the complexity of the postmodern, post-epistemological, post-ideological spirit of the curriculum studies community *as well as* its historic and on-going commitment to democracy as a way of life (Dewey, 1916). Balancing these concerns, we therefore, propose the facilitation of professional development through a narrative inquiry *montage* that is true to Deweyan educational artistry in both method and form and embraces the spirit of Badiou's ethics.

Montage is an aesthetic form that crosses genres. In film, it provides an alternative to cinematic continuity and is a mode of editing in which scenes are juxtaposed in such a way as to create meaning through their collision, conflict, or contradictions. In photography, it describes a process by which multiple photographic images are cut and rejoined to create new images and are sometimes re-photographed to create a seamless image. In audio production, montage refers to the kind of sound collages that are produced through the sampling of portions of existent scores or recordings, from either one or multiple sources, resulting in effects that are something entirely different from the component parts. New technologies in digital film editing, recording, and photography continue to open up novel possibilities for the kinds of combining, rearranging, and synthesis that characterize montage in multiple art forms. Montage, to summarize, is a mode of artistic/intellectual production in which the idea is not necessarily inherent in isolated images, sounds, or ideas, but emerges in the creative fusion of elements.

How might engagement with 'narrative inquiry montage' engender the kinds of ethical commitments that in Badiou's terms are capable of 'bearing new truths', and transforming the current educational 'situation' in powerful ways? Taking up the notion of educational 'artistry' that we have inherited from such luminaries as John Dewey, Joseph Schwab, Maxine Greene, and Eliot Eisner, in order to facilitate this personal journey of understanding we are working with the idea of the 'artist's notebook' as a concrete format for engaging in the artistry of montage. The artist's notebook is a place for musing, for thinking, for playing with ideas. The aim here is to create a 'practitioner-friendly' way of working that is imaginative and fluid, non-procedural, and multi-intelligent (Gardner, 1983)—capable of producing the kinds of epistemological playfulness that we believe the 'complicated conversation' requires, while at the same time, acknowledging the professional importance and serious consequences of educational judgments. We envision the notebook as a professional development tool, used collaboratively or alone to explore the range of ideas in the emerging, evolving curriculum studies canon and draw connections to one's own professional life as an educator in search of democratic wisdom. The notebook would evolve into a professional portfolio that might begin to capture the multi-dimensional, idiosyncratic, and intellectually challenging work of 'becoming democratically wise'.

This 'artist's notebook' would be structured in such a way as to foster meaningful connections between and among the three disciplinary dimensions (verticality, horizonality, diagonality). At the heart of the study process is the individual educator's 'idiosyncratic' journey of understanding. We recognize that the process of evolving to a deeply democratic society is a complex and multi-faceted problem calling forth a number of important dispositions and skills as well as a sophisticated, twenty-first century knowledge base. The artist's notebook is designed to foster these many and varied capacities. We recognize that in a deeply democratic, pluralistic society, differences are not only inherent, but productive, in that, as Dewey foresaw, dealing with difference in a meaningful way advances our collective intelligence. Hence, this approach to professional development is committed to the 'productive idiosyncrasy' of educators, and provides a powerful counter-narrative to the current standardized 'in-servicing' or training models that elicit criticisms from educators who do not feel that their learning needs are being addressed. What distinguishes our approach from more mainstream approaches to professional development is that educators define their own learning needs, in the broad but specific context of becoming more adept at developing students' integrated **S**ubject matter, **S**elf, and **S**ocial knowledge (**3S learning**). Further, in the study/montage format we are working with, educators have a vast array of curriculum disciplinary knowledge to choose from; our 'inquiry map' (see Henderson & Kesson, 2004), which included various modes of curriculum inquiry—craft knowledge, the aesthetic, the dialogic, the critical, the ethical, the political, and the deliberative—is one way of organizing this conceptual territory. Alongside this spectrum of disciplinary knowledge, which Pinar (2007) situates on the vertical axis, educators study the complex, real life situations that constitute the life of schools. The many dimensions of this 'horizontal axis' are articulated in Henderson and Gornik's *Transformative Curriculum Leadership* (2007) and include, as we noted above, reconceptualizing educational standards, building disciplined professional learning communities, exercising public intellectual leadership, deliberative problem-solving, and leadership for systemic change. These are the 'practical arts' that Schwab placed alongside the 'arts of the eclectic'. A conceptual montage is formed through the creative juxtapositions of disciplinary knowledge, practical experiences, and one's own personal journey of understanding, and the conceptual becomes concrete in the artist's notebook, which can include writing, images, or any other expressive forms that seem appropriate.

The images and insights that emerge from this work are key elements in provoking new 'truths' as Badiou would hope; truths that are always born of the specific and concrete but, also, simultaneously, exceed the limits of any particular specific or concrete situation. The focus on the concrete situation precludes indulging in irrelevant abstractions, while the focus on conceptual knowledge ensures the dynamism of the concrete and provokes the transformation of the status quo. Remember that according to Badiou, all truth, and all ethics, must begin with specific cases. It is perhaps here where we can really see the significant connections between Dewey's pragmatism and Badiou's ethics. Here too, we have support for the cultivation of educators' thought and judgment in specific instances or occasions, and by extension, the justification for a situation-specific ethics of curriculum work. This is not, however, an 'anything goes' approach to ethics. On the contrary, we are proposing the ideal of 'deep democracy' as a normative frame, and a disciplined form of curriculum studies-based inquiry to inform the evolving understanding of what it means to practice a 'love of democratic wisdom'.[2]

It is important to understand that we are not presenting a totalizing, definitive, or complete view of what deep democracy is, nor are we providing ethical prescriptions for actions in particular circumstances. The understanding of deep democracy and the ability to exercise wise judgment and right action in particular cases are evolving capacities that constitute a professional development challenge for teachers who wish to engage in ethics-based curriculum work (what we are calling a 'democratic wisdom challenge'). The possibility of ethical fidelity arises when one comes to understand the co-dependency of freedom and responsibility that accompanies a commitment to the path of democratic wisdom. It should be clear from this chapter that this challenge requires an intellectual commitment above and beyond what we have expected from our educators. Concomitant to this intellectual commitment is a demand for increased autonomy over educational decisions as well as a heightened responsibility for educational outcomes. This reflects our sympathy with Dewey's notion of teaching as the 'supreme art' as well as our belief that teaching could become a 'mature profession' (Kesson & Henderson, 2004). As we noted, this process is fraught with complexity, and there are many 'dangers'. Not all educators will welcome this new standard or the challenges that comes with it. To reiterate a point that was made earlier in this chapter, we recognize that we are advancing a 'differentiated' and 'disciplined' professional development approach for self-selected educators who experience a vocational calling to embody and enact democracy-in-education. Our current research on this topic has identified some of the ways that educators either reject or disengage from the necessary internal discipline (Henderson & Gornik, 2008). These educators either see no point to work this hard, or they don't persevere under trying conditions. In effect, they are not cultivating the necessary 'ethical fidelity'.

We hope to see evolve a professional development discourse inspired by the pragmatic and aesthetic ideas of Dewey, and informed by Badiou's ethics; a discourse that elucidates undertheorized concepts such as the event, the situation, multiplicities, immanence, being, and truth procedures. Enacting a philosophically-informed ethical curriculum leadership practice will require us to undertake new ways of knowing, being and acting that embody new professional identities, and to maintain fidelity to strongly held personal values, beliefs and truths. Are we up to the challenge?

Notes

1. The theories of culture-building-through-education ('bildung') that are advanced in the German Didaktic tradition inform this pragmatic consideration (Westbury, Hopmann & Riquarts, 2000).
2. For more on the idea of deep democracy, see Green (1999) and Henderson & Kesson (2004).

References

Aoki, T. (2005) *Curriculum in a New Key: The collected works of Ted T. Aoki* (Mahwah, NJ, Lawrence Erlbaum Associates).

Apple, M. (1988) *Teachers and Texts: A political economy of class and gender relations in education* (New York, Routledge).

Armstrong, K. (2006) *The Great Transformation: The beginning of our religious traditions* (New York, Alfred A. Knopf).

Badiou, A. (2001) *Ethics: An essay on the understanding of evil*, P. Hallward, trans. (London, Verso).

Badiou, A. (2005a) *Being and Event*, O. Feltham, trans. (New York, Continuum). (Original work published 1988)

Badiou, A. (2005b) *Infinite Thought: Truth and the return to philosophy*, O. Feltham & J. Clemens, trans. and eds (London, Continuum).

Badiou, A. (2006) *Theoretical Writings*, R. Brassier & A. Toscano, trans. and eds (London, Continuum).

Cuban, L. (2003) *Why Is It So Hard to Get Good Schools?* (New York, Teachers College Press).

Deleuze, G. (1993) *The Fold: Leibniz and the Baroque*, T. Conley, trans. (Minneapolis, University of Minnesota Press).

Deleuze, G. (1994) *Difference and Repetition*, P. Patton, trans. (New York, Columbia University Press).

Deleuze, G. & Guattari, F. (1987) *A Thousand Plateaus: Capitalism and schizophrenia*, B. Massumi, trans. (Minneapolis, University of Minnesota Press). (Original work published 1980)

Deng, Z. (2007) Transforming the Subject Matter: Examining the intellectual roots of pedagogical content knowledge, *Curriculum Inquiry*, 37:3, 279–295.

Dewey, J. (1916) *Democracy and Education* (New York, The Free Press).

Dewey, J. (1989) *Freedom and Culture* (Buffalo, NY, Prometheus). (Original work published 1939)

Dewey, J. (1998) *Experience and Education* (West Lafayette, IN, Kappa Delta Pi). (Original work published 1938)

Dewey, J. (1999) *Individualism Old and New* (Amherst, NY, Prometheus Books). (Original work published 1929)

Dewey, J. (2004) My Pedagogic Creed, in: D. J. Flinders & S. J. Thornton (eds), *The Curriculum Studies Reader* (2nd edn.) (New York, RoutledgeFalmer), pp. 17–23. (Original work published 1897)

Eisner, E. W. (1994) *The Educational Imagination: On the design and evaluation of school programs* (3rd edn.) (New York, Macmillan).

Fleming, P. (2002) 'Lines of Flight': A History of resistance and the thematic of ethics, death and animality, *Ephemera*, 2:3, 193–208. Available at http://www.ephemeraweb.org.

Ford, G. W. & Pugno, L. (eds) (1964) *The Structure of Knowledge and the Curriculum* (Chicago, Rand McNally & Company).

Foucault, M. (1980) *Power/Knowledge: Selected interviews and other writings 1972–1977*, C. Gordon ed. (New York, Pantheon Books).

Fullan, M. & Hargreaves, A. (1996) *What's Worth Fighting For in Your School?* (New York, Teachers College Press).

Gadamer, H. G. (1975) *Truth and Method*, G. Barden & J. Cumming, eds & trans. (New York, Seabury).

Gardner, H. (1983) *Frames of Mind: The theory of multiple intelligences* (New York, Basic Books).

Garrison, J. (1997) *Dewey and Eros: Wisdom and desire in the art of teaching* (New York, Teachers College Press).

Green, J. M. (1999) *Deep Democracy: Community, Diversity, and Transformation* (Lanham, MD, Rowman & Littlefield).

Greene, M. (1988) *The Dialectic of Freedom* (New York, Teachers College Press).

Henderson, J. G. & Gornik, R. (2007) *Transformative Curriculum Leadership* (3rd edn) (Upper Saddle River, NJ, Merrill/Prentice Hall).

Henderson, J. G. & Gornik, R. (2008) *Report to the Martha Holden Jennings Foundation on the First-Year Pilot Activities for the Creation of a Curriculum Leadership Institute* (Kent, OH, Kent State University).

Henderson, J. G. & Kesson, K. R. (2004) *Curriculum Wisdom: Educational decisions in democratic societies* (Upper Saddle River, NJ, Merrill/Prentice Hall).

Hinchey, P. H. & Cadiero-Kaplan, K. (2005) The Future of Teacher Education and Teaching: Another piece of the privatization puzzle, *Journal for Critical Education Policy Studies*, 3:2. Available at: http://www.jceps.com/index.php?pageID=article&articleID=48.

Jackson, P. W. (2002) *John Dewey and the Philosopher's Task* (New York, Teachers College Press).

Jay, M. (2005) *Songs of Experience: Modern American and European variations on a universal theme* (Berkeley, CA, University of California Press).

Kesson, K. R. & Henderson, J. G. (2004) Cultivating Democratic Curriculum Judgments: Toward a mature profession, in: K. R. Kesson & E. W. Ross (eds), *Defending Public Schools: Teaching for a democratic society* (Westport, CT, Praeger), pp. 3–15.

Kreisberg, S. (1992) *Transforming Power: Domination, Empowerment, and Education* (Albany, NY, SUNY Press).

Kuhn, T. S. (1962) *The Structure of Scientific Revolutions* (Chicago, University of Chicago Press).

Nash, R. J. (2004) *Liberating Scholarly Writing: The Power of Personal Narrative* (New York, Teachers College Press).

Pinar, W. F. (2004) *What is Curriculum Theory?* (Mahwah, NJ, Lawrence Erlbaum Associates).

Pinar, W. F. (2007) *Intellectual Advancement Through Disciplinarity: Verticality and horizontality in curriculum studies* (Rotterdam, Sense Publishers).

Resnick, L. B. (2005) Teaching Teachers: Professional Development to Improve Student Achievement, *Research Points*, 3:1. Available at: http://www.aera.net/uploadedFiles/Journals_and_Publications/Research_Points/RPSummer05.pdf.

Schwab, J. J. (1969) The Practical: A Language for Curriculum, *School Review* 78:1, pp. 1–23.

Uhrmacher, P. B. & Matthews, J. (2005) Building His Palette of Scholarship: A biographical sketch of Elliot Eisner, in: P. B. Uhrmacher & J. Matthews (eds), *Intricate Palette: Working the ideas of Elliot Eisner* (Upper Saddle River, NJ, Merrill/Prentice Hall), pp. 1–13.

van Manen, M. (1991) *The Tact of Teaching: The meaning of pedagogical thoughtfulness* (Albany, NY, SUNY Press).

Westbury, I., Hopman, S. & Riquarts, K. (2000) *Teaching as a Reflective Practice: The German Didaktik tradition* (Mahwah, NJ, Lawrence Erlbaum Associates).

6

The Obliteration of Truth by Management: Badiou, St. Paul and the question of economic managerialism in education

Anna Strhan

Introduction

> The only education is an education *by* truths. (Badiou, 2005, p. 14)
> [T]ruth is a process, and not an illumination. In order to think it, one requires three concepts: one that names the subject at the point of declaration (*pistis* generally translated as 'faith', but which is more appropriately rendered as 'conviction'); one that names the subject at the point of his conviction's militant address (*agapē*, generally translated as 'charity', but more appropriately rendered as 'love'); lastly, one that names the subject according to the force of displacement conferred upon him through the assumption of the truth's procedure's *completed* character (*elpis*, generally translated as 'hope', but more appropriately rendered as 'certainty'). (Badiou, 2003a, p. 15)

Pistis, *agapē*, *elpis*: theological concepts that sound strange, unfamiliar, scandalous within contemporary educational theory and philosophy. Yet, as we see in the quotation above from Alain Badiou's highly provocative *Saint Paul: The Foundation of Universalism*, these concepts assume fundamental significance in his presentation of the nature of truth and subjectivity, fundamental to his conception of what education is. Education, for Badiou, is an education by truths and to think what truth is requires secularizing the concepts of 'conviction', 'love' and 'certainty'. Elsewhere, Badiou describes education as the process of arranging 'the forms of knowledge in such a way that truth may come to pierce a hole in them' (Badiou, 2005, p. 9). What then are we to make of Badiou's notion of education as an education *by* truths, and furthermore, why would such an idea be helpful for thinking about education, given the way that current educational thinking is predominantly structured by concepts such as performance and assessment, or inclusion and the politics of identity? In what follows, I will outline why Badiou's use of Saint Paul provides an opening for an educational discourse that challenges the prevailing hegemony of managerialism and performativity within education. I will consider why this hegemony is problematic, and some of the responses that have been posed to these discourses, for example from the Critical Theory and postcolonial discussion of exclusions and marginalization. After considering why Badiou rejects these discourses, I will show how Badiou's conception of education provides us with an opportunity to re-envision the very nature of educational practice and some of the possible practical implications of this approach.

Why Paul? Weaving New Fabric out of a Ripped Yarn

Given that it is unusual to find the epistles and biography of Saint Paul as the subject of a study by a contemporary philosopher, and possibly even more rare to find reference to a religious saint in a book of educational philosophy, why does *Saint Paul: The Foundation of Universalism* among Badiou's works have any significance for our thinking about the issues of managerialism and performativity within education? In arguably his most vivid and concrete exploration of the process of subjectivity, Badiou shows how Christ's resurrection was for Paul an 'event'. Through the paradigmatic figure of Paul, Badiou considers how the event and the subject's fidelity to it emerge against a background state of a situation. Through comparing Paul's position with our current situation, Badiou reveals the ways in which late capitalism's exchange system is without capacity for truth. This is vital for our understanding of how Badiou's notion of education—as an education by truths—challenges the pedagogical problems related to the dominance of economic managerialism and performativity. Thus, Badiou allows us to consider what truth procedures might mean within a situation of education dominated by the discourses of the market. If these are my reasons for choosing, in this chapter, to question the dominant educational discourses through Badiou's examination of Paul, why does Badiou himself choose to examine Paul?

To allay suspicions of a latent missionary agenda in Badiou's choice of Paul at the outset, it should be emphasized that Badiou is not interested in Paul in relation to theology or religion: 'For me, truth be told, Paul is not an apostle or a saint. I care nothing for the Good News he declares, or the cult dedicated to him' (Badiou, 2003a, p. 1). What he finds of interest in Paul is Paul the 'poet-thinker' reflecting upon what it is to be subject to an event which has ruptured his former ways of thinking and being, his epistles representing his struggle of fidelity to work out what that truth-event means for him and for all. Furthermore, precisely because Paul's faith in the Christ-event is alien to Badiou himself, it allows Badiou to demonstrate that the meaning of the event may only be recognised as constituted by the subject for whom it becomes an event. Simon Critchley puts this point clearly:

> Badiou's choice of Paul as paradigm for the event is all the more compelling because his act of faith is so strange to the modern atheist ... The choice of Paul is intended to show the extreme subject-dependency of the event, that is, that the event is not reducible to the act of a subject, but that the event is only visible as such to the subject who acts in such a way as to pledge themselves to the event. (2005, p. 226)

It is precisely, therefore, *because* the resurrection is a 'fable' for Badiou that it draws attention to the question of belief / faith, 'or that which is presupposed beneath the word *pistis*' (Badiou, 2003a, p. 5). And it is through his exploration of what *pistis* means for Paul that Badiou is able to demonstrate that the Pauline figure of the subject offers genuine revolutionary potential, a potential actualized through his refusal to submit to the order of the existing situation and, in being faithful to the event, his struggle to work and live for a new world. As Badiou argues, Paul's subjectivity in relation to the event of Christ's resurrection demonstrates the necessity to reorganize existing knowledge in light of the event as expressed through his Gospels. Why, however, does Badiou claim that Paul speaks particularly to our *contemporary* situation?

In 'Paul: Our Contemporary', Badiou provides his answer. For Badiou, the significance of Paul can be found in his unprecedented gesture of 'subtracting truth from a communitarian grasp, be that of a people, a city, an empire, a territory, or a social class' (Badiou, 2003a, p. 5). Truth as universal singularity for Badiou is manifest within a world of difference, but cuts through that difference: 'What matters, man or woman, Jew or Greek, slave or free man, is that differences *carry the universal that happens to them like a grace*' (p. 106). Thus, truth as universal singularity, entirely subjective, ruptures and necessitates a reappropriation of prevailing abstractions and particularist protests. For Paul, these were the legal abstractions of being a Roman citizen and the various identities asserted within that realm (even those using particular identities to protest against that realm). Badiou explains the prevailing abstraction that operates for us today in terms of the (false) universality of the rule of the market, subsuming within it even discourses which might appear to subvert it. Ray Brassier (2004) puts this point well:

> Integrated global capitalism is a machine—and a machine is nothing other than an automated axiomatic system—but an astonishingly supple and adaptive one, singularized by its fluidity, its metamorphic plasticity. Whenever confronted by a limit or anomaly, capitalism has the wherewithal—the intelligence?—to invent a new axiom in order to incorporate the unexpected, constantly reconfiguring its parameters by adding a supplementary axiom through which it can continue expanding its own frontiers. (2004, p. 53)

For Badiou, the purely abstracted quantitative universality of monetary exchange is without potential for truths in the realm of political thinking and processes:

> No, we will not allow the rights of true-thought to have as their only instance monetarist free exchange and its mediocre political appendage, capitalist-parliamentarianism, whose squalor is ever more poorly dissimulated behind the fine word 'democracy'. (Badiou, 2003a, p. 7)

Badiou also describes in *Saint Paul* the ways in which the politics of identity and particularist protests are subsumed under the universality of the market. His notion of truth as universal singularity is aimed at exposing what he sees as the deficiency of the cultural and historical relativisations of the question of truth. This he sees as part of the current state of the situation, comparable to the state of the situation for Paul. Truth, and thus thought, he argues, have been reduced 'to a linguistic form, judgment', which rejects this universalism. In this situation, Badiou argues that all forms of the cultural and historical relativisations of the question of truth operate under the abstraction of monetary exchange and the rule of the market, a process he describes as without truth:

> What is the real unifying factor behind this attempt to promote the cultural virtue of oppressed subsets, this invocation of language in order to extol communitarian particularisms (which, besides language, always ultimately refer back to race, religion, or gender)? It is, evidently, monetary abstraction, whose false universality has absolutely no difficulty accommodating the kaleidoscope of communitarianisms. (2003a, pp. 6–7)

The pervasiveness of the rule of the market in the current situation, comparable to Paul's, is all-encompassing. This rule of exchange, the system that seeks to liquidate 'everything substantial according to a rule of universal exchangeability' appears to know no limits, to constantly redefine its boundaries:

> [T]here is an extension of the automatisms of capital, fulfilling one of Marx's inspired predictions: the world finally *configured*, but as a market, as a world-market. This configuration imposes the rule of an abstract homogenization. Everything that circulate falls under the unity of a count, while inversely, only what lets itself be counted in this way can circulate. (2003a, pp. 9–10)

Badiou considers at length the way in which the abstract rule of circulation—'only what counts will be counted: only what can be counted counts'—absorbs within itself the relativist ideology that accompanies the process of fragmentation and differentiation of identity. The creation of differing identities 'creates a figure that provides a material for investment by the market' (p. 10). Indeed, the market requires the appearance of difference or non-equivalence so that the equivalence of exchange can constitute a process. Thus, he provocatively writes:

> What inexhaustible potential for mercantile investments in this upsurge— taking the form of communities demanding recognition and so-called cultural singularities—of women, homosexuals, the disabled, Arabs! And these infinite combinations of predicative traits, what a god-send! Black homosexuals, disabled Serbs, Catholic pedophiles, moderate Muslims, married priests, ecologist yuppies, the submissive unemployed, prematurely aged youth! Each time, a social image authorizes new products, specialized magazines, improved shopping malls, 'free' radio stations ... Deleuze put it perfectly: capitalist deterritorialization requires a constant reterritorialization. (2003a, p. 10)

It is important to note that Badiou is not in any way 'against' difference or the creation of different identities. His criticism of the politics of identity relates to the way in which it leads to particularism and the privileging of some groups over others. He clearly states that difference is the inevitable state of the world: 'in the situation (call it: the world), *there are differences*. One can even maintain that there is nothing else' (p. 98). However, in relation to capitalism, his main contention is that the politics of identity feeds the system of global exchange on the one hand and thereby denies any possibility for the critique of the system on the other. As he asserts, the identities that are configured 'never demand anything but the right to be exposed in the same way as others to the uniform prerogatives of the market' (2003a, p. 11).

This interplay of the homogenization of the global market and the permanent process of the creation of (new) cultural and territorial identities is, for Badiou, without the potential for truths. Indeed, they are *hostile* to truth procedures and this is demonstrated by 'nominal occlusions':

> The name 'culture' comes to obliterate that of 'art'. The word 'technology' obliterates the word 'science'. The word 'management' obliterates the word 'politics'. The word 'sexuality' obliterates love. The 'culture-technology-management-sexuality' system, which has the immense merit of being homogenous to the market, and all of whose terms designate a category of commercial presentation, constitutes the modern nominal occlusion of the 'art-science-politics-love' system, which identifies truth procedures typologically. (2003a, p. 12)

How then is it possible to step outside of the dominant hegemony? Is it possible at all? Badiou provides us with the example of Paul as a 'becoming subject' to truth and shows us how for Paul, the truth of the resurrection, experienced as a universal singularity, pierced through the prevailing abstractions (i.e. Roman Empire) and particularisms of his situation (i.e. Citizen, Jew, Gentile). A truth, according to Badiou, is not structural or legal. And significantly, Badiou argues that a truth cuts through every communitarian subset as a universality. At the same time, a truth is radically subjective in that it is experienced by the subject for who recognises an event as such. Thus, Badiou states:

> Truth is diagonal relative to every communitarian subset; it neither claims authority from, nor (this is obviously the most delicate point) constitutes any identity. It is offered to all, or addressed to everyone, without a condition of belonging being able to limit this offer of this address. (2003a, p. 14)

Conditions of identity clearly do exist, but, as Badiou states, truths are universal and do not belong to any particularist subset of identity or the false universalism of economic exchange.

> [U]ltimately it is a case of mobilizing a universal singularity both against the prevailing abstractions (legal then [in Paul's time], economic now), and against communitarian or particularist protest. (2003a, p. 14)

In relation to Paul as paradigmatic figure for Badiou, such prior conditions of particularist identity and the very categories of knowledge were called into question by the universality of the Christ-event. This is why Paul can proclaim in Galatians 3: 28 'There is neither Jew nor Greek, slave nor free, male nor female, for you are all one in Jesus Christ'. The truth of the event and the practical working out of what fidelity to that event means as the process of subjectivity, displaces the subject from these legal abstractions, particularisms of identity and the apparatus of opinion. Likewise, in relation to our contemporary situation, truth as universal singularity cannot belong to the count of capitalism. The truth of the event is here 'entirely subjective (it is of the order of a declaration that testifies to a conviction relative to the event)' (2003a, p. 14): for Paul, the truth event of the resurrection is not established through what would have been for him the 'objective' categories of Jewish Law or Greek Logos, and indeed, the Christ-event leads renders these laws obsolete if not harmful. So, as stated, it is not Paul's message that Badiou sees as harbouring potential for delineating the nature of subjectivity, but rather Paul the subject who has experienced the Christ-event as entirely subjective and yet universal in its appeal; an event that necessitates a radical break from within the structures of knowledge and identity that define existing situations.

What then does this mean for education? In *Handbook of Inaesthetics*, Badiou links education to the event of truth disrupting the established forms of knowledge and the state of the situation:

> '[E]ducation' (save in its oppressive or perverted expressions) has never meant anything but this: to arrange the forms of knowledge in such a way that truth may come to pierce a hole in them. (2005, p. 9)

He elaborates further:

> [T]he only education is an education by truths. (2005, p. 14)

In other words, according to Badiou, education references a process of subjectivity in that education involves truth piercing through established forms of knowledges and the subject's subsequent re-appropriation of those structures of knowledge in light of the event. Here, truth and, by implication, education, are processes rather than illuminations: 'now we see only in a glass darkly' (1 Corinthians 13:12). A truth-procedure is the practical working out of what fidelity to the event means, a process both instituted in the event and yet still being worked out. It is fidelity to the event that is the process of subjectivity. The event itself is not a teaching or something that can be known, but is rather pure gift, 'a kind of laicized grace' (Hallward, 2003, p. 115).

The subject is thus, for Badiou, 'constituted by evental grace' (Badiou, 2003a, p. 63): the event and its truth cannot be contained within the rule of exchange and the market and indeed grace bursts asunder the economy of monetary exchange. The event is pure contingent gift and not something that could be demanded or the result of my own action, and cannot be contained even by thought: 'Thought can be raised up from its powerlessness only through something that exceeds the order of thought' (2003a, pp. 84–85). It is important to note that this is not simply a secular colonisation of the Christian tradition in terms of the old 'true/false consciousness' debate in Marxism: 'Know the truth and the truth will set you free'. No: Paul is paradigmatic for Badiou because he illustrates the entirely subjective nature of the event as that which is both a singularity and a universal. It is a singularity because it could only occur in particular circumstances, but universal in that the implications of the event are lived in the name of and for all. Badiou's discussion of Paul's articulation of the meaning of the event for him shows that truth-procedures involve the radical reassessment of our inherited forms of knowledge. Subjectivity—as the working out of the conditions of fidelity to an event—cannot simply be reduced to a true/false dichotomy.

It is important to emphasise that the event here is not the reification of some sort of epiphany, comparable to a road to Emmaus type experience. In *Ethics* (2001), Badiou gives a useful clarification of what we are to understand by the terms event, fidelity and truth as he uses them:

> The three major dimensions of a truth-process are as follows:
> * the *event*, which brings to pass 'something other' than the situation, opinions, instituted knowledges; the event is a hazardous, unpredictable supplement, which vanishes as soon as it appears;
> * the *fidelity*, which is the name of the process: it amounts to a sustained investigation of the situation, under the imperative of the event itself; it is an immanent and continuing break;
> * the *truth* as such, that is, the multiple, internal to the situation, that the fidelity constructs, bit by bit; it is what the fidelity gathers together and produces. (2001, pp. 67–68)

Badiou goes on, in *Ethics*, to discuss the Haydn-event in classical music as a concrete example of these terms useful for thinking through their application to education. The event is ontologically situated: with the Haydn-event, the emergence of the classical style takes place in a situation governed by the baroque style. The event reveals the void at the heart of the state of the current situation, a void that could not be perceived within the state of the situation prior to the event. Within the baroque style, the void, according to Badiou, was 'the absence [*vide*] of a genuine conception of musical architectonics. The Haydn-event occurs as a kind of naming of this absence' (2001, p. 68). The event then necessitates the reordering of the knowledges that have been disrupted by the event, which is the construction of truth. Following the Haydn-event, new musical knowledge was organised around the classical style, knowledge that could not have been formulated prior to this event. This reorganisation of knowledges subsequent to the event Badiou describes as the forcing of knowledges:

> A truth punches a 'hole' in knowledges, it is heterogenous to them, but it is also the sole known source of new knowledges. We shall say that the truth *forces* knowledges. The verb *to force* indicates that since the power of a truth is that of a break, it is by violating established and circulating knowledges that a truth returns to the immediacy of the situation, or reworks that sort of portable encyclopaedia from which opinions, communications and sociality draw their meaning. If a truth is never communicable as such, it nevertheless implies, at a distance from itself, powerful reshapings of the forms and referents of communication. (2001, p. 70)

Although knowledges are forced by the event, and the truth procedure takes place through the reworking of new knowledges in the immediacy of the situation, the event itself is a grace that could not be forced. In response to this gift, the working out of the conditions of fidelity to the event in which I become a subject, I am an agent of change. The subject then emerges in the process of subjectivization, the transformation that takes place through the actions of the individual in response to the event that took place, which was, for them, a gift. The investigation by the subject of the consequences of the event that occurred and disrupted the economy of exchange as pure gift, as Feltham and Clemens note, 'entails not only the active transformation of the situation in which the event occurs but also the active transformation of the situation of the human being' (cited in Badiou, 2003c, p. 7). Thus education, in *this* view, entails this process of a transformation that necessarily breaks the closed totality of the economy of monetary exchange.

Within this conception of subjectivity the subject needs to re-appropriate the meaning of the structures that have been disrupted by the truth procedure in 'not ... but,' articulation. This is to weave a new fabric out of the ripped yarn of the situation. Eric Santner describes this idea clearly:

> [H]uman subjects undergo tears in the fabric of their lives, tears that, in principle, allow not simply for new choices of objects of desire, but rather for the radical restructuring of the coordinates of desire, for genuine changes of direction in life. Ethical consistency will mean something like the creation of new fabric *out of a tear*. (Santner, 2005, p. 110)

This idea raises the question of the extent to which formal education, as currently woven with the yarns of economic managerialism, performativity and marketisation, might allow truth to break through and the subject to weave new fabrics with their lives. If education, according to Badiou's definition, involves the tearing and breaking of the current coordinates of the state of the situation, to what extent is this actually possible within the current environment dominated by market policy?

The Economy of Exchange and the Marketization and Customerisation of Education

> I'm only here [at school] to get good enough grades to go a good university, so that I can get a good job and earn decent money one day. And it's the teacher's job to make sure I get those grades.

These words, spoken to me by a 17-year-old student at a school in an affluent area of west London over five years ago, could be seen as reflecting the pervasiveness of the 'customerisation' of teaching and learning, stemming from the prevailing ideologies of marketisation and managerialism within education. This student saw the school as the provider of his education, reflected in the 'good grades' he desired that would enable him to achieve his career goal of 'earning decent money'. The application of business models leading to a managerialistic approach to the organisation of formal education, with an emphasis on production-oriented service delivery is already well documented (Clarke, Gewirtz & McLaughlin, 2000; Apple, 2001;

Preston, 2001; Bridges & Jonathan, 2003; Love, 2008). Even if such language sits uneasily with many, it is now commonplace for students or their parents to be described as the 'consumers' of education (the product), which is 'delivered' by the 'providers' (schools, universities). Bridges and Jonathan give several examples to demonstrate how in the UK, for example, the Labour government has shown just as great an enthusiasm for the application of market principles to education as its Tory predecessors:

> ... extending rather than limiting parental choice of schools and the assessment and league tables that are supposed to inform such choice; enabling popular schools to expand; introducing student fees in the context of higher education, and showing some favor toward universities that wish to introduce differential charging; and taking on teachers' unions in a battle over performance-related pay. (Bridges & Jonathan, 2003, p. 126)

They describe the conditions for this 'marketization' of education as the creation of diversity and choice and the placing of information and purchasing power in the hands of the 'consumer'. This process of the marketisation of education has been widely documented across North America and in Britain, but is no longer solely a feature of the Anglo-American liberal conservatism. Bridges and Jonathan point out that 'regimes in such diverse political environments as Russia, Ethiopia and Vietnam are all sending government ministers and officials on courses in market economics and wrestling with the application of market principles to social policy' (p. 127), and a number of international bodies, such as Organisation for Economic Co-operation and Development, International Monetary Fund and World Bank have all supported policies associated with managerialism. The application of market principles has led to the widespread dominance of economic managerialism within education. Tom Woodin (2008) suggests that the concept of managerialism implies the over-use of managers and management techniques, particularly in the public services. The notion depends on the idea that social, economic, political and cultural issues can be solved through better management according to certain key principles of management technique, such as emphasis on target setting and achievement. Thus, management is seen to lead to value for money, efficiency and improved customer service.

Essential to managerialism, as Preston (2001) outlines, is the ability to meet quality / performance targets, as part of an 'Audit Society' or Foucault's surveillance society (Foucault, 1991), in which all activities that can be measured and assessed ought to be measured and assessed. In Britain, for example, schools now use 'value-added' scores to assess the quality of a student's grades relative to the initial 'input' of the student's ability. As Preston writes, 'the accuracy of the word processor and the health of our school children are reduced to the same Ethic of Effectiveness, a Quality good with value-added components' (Preston, 2001, p. 348). The desire for information and norms against which to assess quality within education reflects a wider desire for information and feedback by which to judge the quality of service provision within society. In Britain, we have league table rankings of just about every 'service' in which 'consumer' choice is possible, from restaurants and hotels, now to schools, universities and even hospitals. Within British schools, the 'performance' of individuals teachers is assessed through spreadsheets of their students' exam grades and observations by external examining bodies, while in some British schools, teachers are required to enter all their lesson plans into the school network so that the senior management can monitor that they are planned to meet the criteria of 'the model lesson'. All of these factors have had a significant impact on the degree to which teachers feel they can exercise curricular autonomy and many feel stifled by this rhetoric of the market. By this, I do not mean to imply that the practice of auditing in itself, through examination, observation, inspection and other means of assessment, is necessarily forbidding. It is clearly necessary in some ways. The problem outlined by Preston and others is that audit as an idea overreaches its originally financial aim of ensuring that the money spent on education is delivering quality. Thus the process of audit becomes institutionalised as an entire principle of social organisation, leading to a state of constant vigilance within educational systems and within society as a whole.

It is beyond the scope of this chapter to examine the complex reasons lying behind the rise of the discourses of managerialism, performativity and marketisation within education. Although a shared concern for value for money and efficiency might explain the application of market principles in different educational contexts, it is worth noting that educational theorists have outlined different ideological reasons underlying the rise of managerial models. In Britain, for example, studies of the use of the managerial model within public services by New Labour have suggested that this can be linked to a desire to bring about greater democracy and inclusion. Jenny Ozga outlines this position:

> New Labour's modernization of education, which uses managerialism as its vehicle ... [seeks] to create an enterprising culture of the system, the institution and the self. It privileges waged work as the passport to inclusion, as well as the creation of wealth (common and individual) and in so doing it seeks to remove the need for separate recognition of the social and cultural work that education does, because that is now encompassed within programmes that promote achievement. The pursuit of achievement is the route to employment but it is also the means of ensuring appropriate socialization and cultural integration. (Ozga, 2000, pp. 222–23)

The emphasis here on the deployment of a managerial model of education in order to seek fuller inclusion differs from what Michael Apple sees as the ideology lying behind similar practices and discourses in the US, which he links to a shift to the right in education policy, guided by a neoliberal vision of the weak state:

> What is private is necessarily good and what is public is necessarily bad. Public institutions such as schools are 'black holes' into which money is poured—and then seemingly disappears—but which do not provide anywhere near adequate results. For neoliberals, one form of rationality is more powerful than any other—economic rationality. Efficiency and an 'ethic' of cost-benefit analysis are the dominant norms. (Apple, 2001, p. 38)

However, both Apple and Ozga's analyses of British and American systems of education—as driven by the rhetoric of efficiency—imply a shared underlying aim of education: to prepare students for economic participation in society. Students are thus seen as human capital: 'The world is intensely competitive economically, and students—as future workers—must be given the requisite skills and dispositions to compete efficiently and effectively' (Apple, 2001, p. 38). Thus the marketisation of education is seen by neoliberals, according to Apple, as necessary to prevent schools from 'sucking the financial life out of society' and ensuring that students as human capital are prepared for paid work. Crucial to this, Apple argues, is the idea of the 'consumer':

> For neoliberals, the world in essence is a vast supermarket. 'Consumer choice' is the guarantor of democracy. In effect, education is seen as simply one more product like bread, cars, and television. By turning it over to the market through voucher and choice plans, education will be largely self-regulating. Thus, democracy is turned into consumption practices. (Apple, 2001, p. 39)

We can see, then, that underlying both these ideologies of managerialism is the view that education is conceived instrumentally as a vehicle for participation in waged work and reproducing the current state of the situation as ruled by the principle of monetary exchange. And this is achieved through the application of models of performativity and auditing in order to ensure that value for money is being achieved in the provision of education and that students emerge from education ready to earn capital. The various negative consequences of these processes have been documented as leading in some situations to the social and economic exclusion of those who do not succeed within the standardised testing system, while also leading to dissatisfaction among teachers and a strangling of thought. Fred Inglis writes of the emphasis on auditing within the managerial structures of British schools and universities:

> The preposterous edifice of auditing, the mad rout of acronyms—HEFCE, TQM, OFSTED, TTA—blinds vision and stifles thought. Their most certain consequence is to make inquiry servile, knowledge instrumental, and, above all, to make all of us, teachers at whatever level, boring, exhausted and hating the job. (Inglis, 2000, p. 429)

Before we turn to examine how Badiou's notions of education, truth and subjectivity can help us think outside of the prevailing ideologies and re-envision the emancipatory potential of education, let us first briefly consider the standard responses to the management problematic from educational theorists working within the discourses of Critical Theory and, linked to this, the so-called 'politics of identity'.

The Rule of the Market Under Attack

Given the history of Critical Theory related to Marxism, albeit having travelled a significant distance from its roots, it is not surprising to find analyses of capitalist schooling as instruments of corporate power and domination coming from those working within this tradition. Within such approaches, there remains a commitment from Marxism to a liberation from 'false consciousness', although not in the original Marxist formulation of that idea. In examining current hegemonic discourses within education, those who have been influenced by Critical Theory tend therefore to have a transformative vision of the potential of an education that does not seek to reproduce existing inequalities and social divisions, but rather one that might empower groups who are marginalised within society and thereby lead to greater democracy. This approach is exemplified in Michael Apple's attack on US education policy. He places race at the centre of his attempted interruption of the hegemony of the marketisation of education, focusing on how existing schooling systems with their emphasis on standardised testing have the result of excluding those with least access to economic, social and cultural capital. His argument is for a politics of recognition that will challenge the inequalities that are reproduced within the current systems of education: it is 'not possible to be color-blind ... only by noticing race can we challenge it ... By placing race squarely in front of us', we can challenge 'the state, the institutions of civil society, and ourselves as individuals to combat the legacy of inequality and injustice inherited from the past' (Apple, 2001, pp. 203–204). Education, in this view, could and should offer up a space for considering key issues involved in the politics of representation and diversity. Apple describes his critique as part of the politics of identity, but is critical of previous theorists of identity for not going far enough in attacking the conservative policies he describes as underlying the hegemonies of marketisation and performativity within education:

> This is partly an issue of the politics of 'identity', and increasing attention has been paid over the past decade to questions of identity in education and cultural studies. However, one of the major failures of research on identity is its failure to adequately address the hegemonic politics of the right. As I have been at pains to show here and elsewhere, the conservative restoration has been more than a little successful in creating active subject positions that incorporate varied groups under the umbrella of a new hegemonic alliance. It has been able to engage in a politics inside and outside of education in which a fear of the racialized Other is connected to fears of nation, culture, control and decline—and to intensely personal fears about the future of one's children in an economy in crisis. (Apple, 2001, p. 211)

Critiques drawn from Critical Theory that include multiculturalist problematics in the interests of radical democracy have been put forward by several other prominent educational theorists, such as Henry Giroux (1983) and Carlos Torres (1998). Giroux has, however, stressed the importance of moving from critique to a discourse of hope: that there are ways of resisting the imposition of market and business models within education by emphasizing the role that schools potentially play as spaces in which a false consciousness might be dissolved, leading to a positively formulated vision of democracy.

Another type of criticism that has been posed to the culture of managerialism and the market in education comes from those theorists who emphasise the importance of personal well-being. John White is an exponent of such a position. In 'Education, the Market and the Nature of Personal Well-Being' (2005), he outlines educating students to lead personally fulfilling lives as a key aim of education. He points out that the market *can* bring with it goods that help an individual to live a flourishing life, suggesting:

> The market, in opening up its own range of options to meet the consumer's autonomous preferences, reinforces the implicit messages about personal well-being that the educational bodies have been transmitting. (White, 2005, p. 100)

However, the values of the market must always, according to White, be seen 'in the light of wisdom already accumulated within the culture about what makes for a flourishing life' (p. 107). Thus, the rule of the market within education might be challenged if it does not tie in with what White describes as collective wisdom about what contributes to human flourishing.

Given then that there have already been numerous critical responses to the rule of market and managerialism within education, what does Badiou add to our understanding of this problematic? It is clear that we can recognise what Badiou describes as our current state of the situation in *Saint Paul* as also the state of the situation in education. Let us briefly remind ourselves of how Badiou summarised the state of the contemporary situation:

> Our world is in no way as 'complex' as those who wish to ensure its perpetuation claim. It is even, in its broad outline, perfectly simple. On the one hand, there is an extension of the automatisms of capital, fulfilling one of Marx's inspired predictions: the world finally *configured*, but as a market, as a world-market ... On the other side, there is a process of fragmentation into closed identities, and the culturalist and relativist ideology that accompanies this fragmentation. (Badiou, 2003a, pp. 9–10)

It is easy to recognize this as the state of the situation in education, subsumed within abstract homogenization of monetary exchange through the imposition of market principles as I have outlined above. And although Badiou does not extensively treat the subject of education policy, in an interview he does comment on how the French have followed British policy in applying the principles of the market to education which the State defends using the 'propaganda' of economic necessity:

> [E]very State uses propaganda to convince us that all the decisions they take are necessary. Let us take for instance the French government (although the same could be said about the British government). What is the French government saying to us? As the British government before, it is destroying public hospitals, public schools etc. It follows the British and follow it will. What is the State explaining? It is explaining that specific policies *must* be implemented ... [T]hey claim that such policies

are mandatory. But is this truly the case? It is his policy to say that it is necessary, it is the State policy. This is the government's way of situating this State policy in an economical context that is part of State decisions. (Badiou, 2003b, p. 189)

It seems then, that Badiou himself might suggest that a politics of decision-making in education have been replaced by management: education policy comes to be defended by reference to economic 'necessity' rather than any other criteria. Thus, education is absorbed by the rule of the market in order to facilitate its better functioning. Within education policy, we have seen the pervasiveness of management, indeed the replacement of politics by management. The structures of management do not allow the question of truth into discussions about how formal education should be organised or about what education is or should be. All, as Badiou suggests, can only be explained with reference to economic necessity. In this way, the question of truths in education becomes obliterated by management premised on an alleged requirement of necessity.

What becomes evident is that the responses from Critical Theory also fall within this state of necessity requiring managerial approaches that deny any discussion of truths—one that accepts identifications as the problem to be solved via access to the count of the market, a problem that can rectified by 'proper' economic distributions and recognitions. We have already discussed how Badiou sees this situation and its allegedly critical contestations as without the potential for truths. According to Badiou, therefore, '[t]he capitalist logic of the general equivalent and the identitarian and cultural logic of communities or minorities form an articulated whole' (2003a, p. 11). Thus we might say that both the imposition of economic managerialism within education and the responses from critical theory form part of what Badiou has outlined as our contemporary situation. What is particularly significant therefore about Badiou's challenge for education is that he alerts our attention to and steers us between the Scylla of economic management and the Charybdis of an identitarian politics that can lead to bigotry. As Peter Hallward argues:

> We live in supremely reactionary times. Ours is a moment in which inventive politics has been replaced with economic management, in which the global market has emerged as the exclusive mechanism of social coordination. Ours is a moment in which effective alternatives to this mechanism find expression almost exclusively in the bigotries of culturally specified groups or identities, from ultranationalism in Germany and France to competing fundamentalisms in Israel and Algeria. Among contemporary thinkers, Badiou stands alone in the uncompromising rigor of his confrontation with these twin phenomena. (2003, p. xxxvi)

Having therefore shown that Badiou's outline of the state of the situation in *Saint Paul* is a situation we recognise within current educational discourses and institutions, how is that his notion of education as an education by truths helps us to re-envision the nature of education in a way that can be mobilised against the distortion of education by managerialism?

Is Education Possible in Schools?

We have already considered Badiou's interpretation of education as an education by truths. But what might this mean in more practical terms? In a recent interview with Oliver Feltham, Badiou makes the following comment upon the organisation of schooling:

> Junior high school should be abolished: between eleven and fifteen years old all young people without exception should be integrated into productive work, with perhaps half the time spent studying, or a quarter. They will come back to full-time study once they are sixteen years old, having all acquired a tenacious 'worker' configuration. These later studies will not decide their future but provide an initiation to truth procedures. (Badiou, 2008, p. 138)

This point is worth pondering, particularly given the fact that Badiou has worked within systems of education, as both school teacher and within a university, through-out his career. Is Badiou serious, and if so, what would be the purpose of such a radical rethinking of education policy? Furthermore, how does this relate to Badiou's theorization of the nature of education? Before we answer these questions, I would like to draw attention to a criticism made by Nigel Blake and Jan Masschelein about the use of Critical Theory within educational theory:

> Like its European counterparts, American critical pedagogy remains attached to a strongly instrumental and functional concept of educational practice, because it has not questioned the very concept of educational *praxis* itself but conceived it as an *instrument* for liberation or repression. Educational *praxis* still receives its meaning from the goal or end at which it should aim ... Critical pedagogy thus formulates essentially and fundamentally a technological project. Its first step is the formulation of an ideal or utopia, which it uncritically supposes both possible and necessary. It thus remains itself subject to the same instrumental logic that it deplores at the heart of the capitalist system. (Blake & Masschelein, 2003, p. 50)

The same criticism could also clearly be directed against the managerial model of education (aiming to reproduce the dominant hegemony and to maximise the creation of capital) and the personal well-being model (aiming at a utopian vision of human flourishing). I do not wish, in saying this, to disparage the ideal of a utopian inclusive democratic state, or the aim of enhancing students' flourishing. But Blake and Masschelein's criticism of the notion of education in critical pedagogy serves to highlight what is particularly distinctive in Badiou's presentation: its anti-instrumentalism.

   We might say that Badiou's notion of education as an education by truths is at its very core anti-instrumentalist. School should not be a place for preparing people for work, but rather a site of 'initiation into truth procedures'. The challenge of Badiou is therefore a radical one: to see structures of education not as a place for preparing people for economic participation, but rather as sites that might enable the beginning of the processes of subjectivity, introducing students to past events and enabling them, potentially, to begin to work out what fidelity to past events might mean, just as teachers are also struggling to work out the conditions of fidelity. It would be impossible to plan for events within education. As Badiou states: 'it is of the essence of the event not to be preceded by any sign, and to catch us unawares with its grace, regardless of our vigilance' (2003a, p. 111). However, even if we can't wait for events to happen we can still be working out the conditions of fidelity to past events:

> Many events, even very distant ones, still require us to be faithful to them. Thought does not wait, and it has never exhausted its reserve of power, unless it be for him who succumbs to the profound desire to conform, which is the path of death. (p. 111)

Oliver Feltham provides a helpful example to illustrate this idea:

> There are high-school teachers in France who try to educate students in line with the maxim inscribed over the front door of every public school: *liberté, egalité, fraternité*. These teachers are still trying to work out just what the French revolution is, and what it entails, in the field of education. The French revolution is not yet closed. *Aux armes citoyens!* The revolution is not yet over. (Feltham, 2008, p. 103)

Badiou's call for us to be faithful to past events in the current situation requires that the current situation be read in the light of such events; a reflection difficult to read given the invisible abstract universalization of the market count to which education is accountable in contemporary situations.

The challenge of Badiou therefore is to recover education as a space for what he describes as 'true-thought', which means a thinking that has not been colonised by the processes of managerialism and performativity, and therefore might provide emancipation from and challenges to these discourses. The current state of the situation in education does not count students as capable of thought. Hallward puts this point well:

> Badiou's presumption is that by itself no ordinary situation ever really counts its members as thinking beings, i.e. in terms that respect those indefinable or inconsistent qualities that allow them to *think*, precisely— their immeasurable potential, their affirmative intensity, their infinite capacity for inspiration, and so on. Only rarely does it happen that people act not as objects evaluated by an employer, an educator or a friend, but as participants in one of the few possible fields in which pure affirmation is possible (in the fields of politics, art, science or love). For a truth to proceed in an employment situation, for instance, the criteria normally deployed to distinguish employers from employees, and profitable employees from unprofitable ones, would somehow have to be suspended in an affirmation or generic equality. (Hallward, 2004, p. 7)

Badiou's radical proposal of a system of education that is divorced from preparing students for waged work might allow for students to be initiated into truth-procedures and to recognise and respect them as thinking beings. There is not space here to consider what this would mean in terms of curriculum planning for this later stage of education as initiation into truth-procedures that Badiou proposes. However, his comments in *Saint Paul* that truth procedures within the fields of art, politics, science and love having been obliterated by the 'culture-technology-management-sexuality' system might help us to think about what would and what would not be desirable when planning educational curricula (Badiou, 2003a, p. 12).

However, Badiou's proposal for a system of education from age sixteen which is not a preparation for work but rather the site of initiation into truth procedures is likely to be dismissed by most educational theorists as unworkable. Joseph Dunne for example explains very clearly why it is so difficult to divorce education from utilitarian economic concerns, as Badiou seems to advocate:

> The relationship between education and the economy has become a reciprocal one, with dependency running in both directions. On the one hand, the productiveness of the economy depends on the educational system for the supply of a skilled workforce (what is increasingly called 'human capital'). On the other hand, the educational system depends on a productive economy for funding on the scale which is required by a modern democratic system of schooling ... This interlocking of education with the productive and economic sphere circumscribes the autonomy of education, rendering problematic the ideal of a humanistic education without utilitarian purpose. (Dunne, 2005, p. 149)

Given then that the rule of economic necessity, as suggested by Dunne, dictates that it is highly unlikely that Badiou's proposal will come to pass, and there may be other reasons for opposition to his proposal. What can be done within current state of the situation to enable education to become a potential site for the initiation into truth procedures?

As a teacher, I feel challenged by Badiou to create situations for my students to encounter past events and consider what it would mean to be faithful to those events today. I want to allow them the opportunity to see the universality of the rule of the market as a situation without capacity for truths, and consider Badiou's challenge that the truth domains of art, science, politics and love are occluded and indeed obliterated by the culture-technology-management-sexuality system. And so, as I reflect upon my experience as a teacher, Badiou's writing speaks to me of the urgent need for the recovery of the following concepts within education: space and grace. I do not choose these terms because of a convenient assonance. 'Space' is a familiar term to be considering within education, while 'grace' sounds scandalous within the secular discourses of education with which we are familiar. Badiou encourages us to think of both terms in quite specific ways, so that their meaning exceeds how the terms have been conventionally used. While I will outline each only briefly, they both invite further attention.

Space

In answering a question about his own struggle against the State apparatus, Badiou suggests that in order to oppose the ever-extending forces of the global capitalist machine, what is needed is space within which to think and develop one's own methods of opposition:

> We need a strategy that allows us to create our own space, to develop our own strategies and political decisions. The question of space is fundamental to politics ... And political independence is to be able to choose your own space. (Badiou, 2003b, p. 189)

In relation to education, teachers are not allowed this space to question that is needed for political independence. The culture of economic managerialism that seeks to preserve and extend the capitalist hegemony does not provide opportunity for teachers to deviate from the accepted norms of discourse or even space for teachers to question those norms. My teacher training (and it is significant that the very idea of 'teacher education' has been occluded by 'teacher training') followed, as is the norm, an apprenticeship model, in which I learnt to make model lesson plans, write schemes of work, the overriding importance of assessment. Of course, all of these are important skills within teaching, but there was no space given to questioning or exploring the political implications and ideologies behind the systems into which we were being initiated. And in my subsequent experience of teaching, I have seen little opportunity afforded to teachers to reflect upon and question their place within the prevailing abstractions that dominate educational discourses. In short, many teachers are initiated into and live in common places without space to potentially access their potentials to engage in truth-processes. Badiou's critique suggests that if education is to be attentive to the question of truth, then space needs to be opened up for the possibility of thinking and acting that cannot be contained within logics derived from the economy of exchange. As it is with teachers so it needs to be for students. Each require space to think at a distance to the prevailing abstractions of the state of the situation; to consider, for example, the nature of past events and how these emerged against and disrupted previous situations and discourses. This is, therefore, not just a space that is required to think and reflect on one's practice, but rather space as the condition for the initiation into truth-procedures and for the possibility of *true-thought*, the possibility of live thought.

Grace

> 'Grace' means that thought cannot *wholly* account for the brutal starting over on the path of life in the subject, which is to say, for the rediscovered conjunction between thinking and doing. Thought can be raised up from its powerlessness only through something that exceeds the order of thought. 'Grace' names the event as condition for an active thought. The condition is itself inevitably in excess of what it conditions. (Badiou, 2003a, pp. 84–85)

The significance of grace within Badiou's conception of truth-procedures can be seen as exposing the impoverishment of the type of thinking that can be contained, packaged, delivered and its quality assessed within current educational systems. Thought, as Badiou suggests, can only become powerful through that which exceeds the very nature of thought. Standish (2005) has argued that what is missing within the dominance of the economy of exchange is an 'economy of excess'. This he explores in relation to the significance of alterity and infinity in the thinking of Levinas. Within an economy of excess, education takes on a different character from the closed totality of exchange in which all learning can be planned for and assessed, according to the dictate of managerial approaches. Perhaps rather than focusing on developing transferable skills, acquiring subject matter content is best achieved in the service of what the subject seeks to know more of. In an economy of excess,

> ... a subject of study comes be to understood as deepening and expanding the more one pursues it: as with the vista that extends as one ascends the mountainside, one progresses towards a greater understanding of what there is still to learn ... There is nothing fanciful about this: this is the familiar experience of people who love their subjects; and against it so many aspects of current policy and practice, and of the prevailing discourse of teaching, learning and research methods, look palely narcissistic. (Standish, 2005, p. 52)

While limited by dominant logics, those moments of experiencing the subject under study deepening and extending that Standish describes as an economy of excess *do* happen within education. I have seen my students, and indeed myself as a student, become absorbed and changed by the texts and ideas under study. The truth of a play, a novel, a poem, *can* be manifest in the setting of formal education. And in *Saint Paul,* Badiou challenges the reader to consider the humility of such a mani-fested encounter:

> Whoever is the subject of a truth (of love, of art, or science, or politics) knows that, in effect, he bears a treasure, that he is traversed by an infinite power. Whether or not this truth, so precarious, continues to deploy itself depends solely on his subjective weakness. Thus, one may justifiably say that he bears it only in an earthen vessel. (Badiou, 2003a, p. 54)

Thus, as teachers, if we are to see our role as helping students to encounter truth-procedures, we are challenged to assist them to see the truths they encounter as precious, fragile and dependent on those who recognise past 'events' as continuing to exist as truths. All of this raises questions about curricular autonomy and the role of the teacher in these procedures which demand further attention in the light of Badiou's challenge.

The event, as pure gift, could never be bought or exchanged. Despite the tendency of the managerialistic approach to abduct truth from the proceedings of education, it is still there, even if occluded, in the subjectivity of those who *are* working out fidelity to past events in such a way as new events might take place. The challenge of Badiou is therefore to be watchful and resist the tendency of the law of the count and the principle of (monetary) exchange to foreclose the possibility of live thought. As educators we must be aware that the current configuration of the education as measurable and deliverable misses the richness of education as the possible site of eventual grace. The one who is educated is *not* learning only in order to get good enough grades to get a good job. They are also potentially in the process of becoming subjects to truths and so agents of change. As educationalists, we must not allow the seeming obliteration of truth by management to hide this.

References

Apple, M. W. (2001) *Educating the 'Right' Way: Markets, standards, God, and inequality* (New York & London, Routledge Falmer).

Badiou, A. (2001) *Ethics: An essay on the understanding of evil*, P. Hallward, trans. (London & New York, Verso).

Badiou, A. (2003a) *Saint Paul: The foundation of universalism*, R. Brassier, trans. (Stanford, CA, Stanford University Press).

Badiou, A. (2003b) After the Event: Rationality and the politics of invention. An interview with Alain Badiou conducted by the Radical Politics group at the University of Essex, *Prelom Koletiv: Journal for Images and Politics*, 8, pp. 180–197.

Badiou, A. (2003c) *Infinite Thought: Truth and the return to philosophy*, O. Feltham and J. Clemens, trans. (London and New York, Continuum).

Badiou, A. (2005) *Handbook of Inaesthetics*, A. Toscano trans. (Stanford, CA, Stanford University Press).

Badiou, A. (2008) 'Live Badiou', an interview with Alain Badiou, in: O. Feltham (ed.), *Alain Badiou: Live theory* (London & New York, Continuum), pp. 136–139.

Blake, N. & Masschelein, J. (2003) Critical Theory and Critical Pedagogy, in: N. Blake, P. Smeyers, R. Smith & P. Standish (eds), *The Blackwell Guide to the Philosophy of Education* (Oxford, Blackwell), pp. 38–56.

Brassier, R. (2004) Nihil Unbound: Remarks on subtractive ontology and thinking capitalism, in: P. Hallward (ed.), *Think Again: Alain Badiou and the future of philosophy* (London & New York, Continuum), pp. 50–58.

Bridges, D. & Jonathan, R. (2003) Education and the Market, in: N. Blake, P. Smeyers, R. Smith & P. Standish (eds), *The Blackwell Guide to the Philosophy of Education* (Oxford, Blackwell), pp. 126–145.

Clarke, J., Gewirtz, S. & McLaughlin, E. (eds) (2000) *New Managerialism New Welfare?* (London, Sage).

Critchley, S. (2005) On the Ethics of Alain Badiou, in: G. Riera (ed.), *Alain Badiou: Philosophy and its conditions* (Albany, State University of New York Press), pp. 215–236.

Dunne, J. (2005) What's the Good of Education?, in: W. Carr (ed.), *The RoutledgeFalmer Reader in Philosophy of Education* (Oxford & New York, Routledge), pp. 145–160.

Feltham, O. (2008) *Alain Badiou: Live theory* (London & New York, Continuum).

Foucault, M. (1991) *Discipline and Punish*, A. Sheridan, trans. (London, Penguin).

Giroux, H. (1983) *Theory and Resistance in Education: A pedagogy for the opposition* (London, Heinemann).

Hallward, P. (2003) *Badiou: A subject to truth* (Minneapolis, University of Minnesota Press).

Hallward, P. (2004) *Think Again: Alain Badiou and the future of philosophy* (London & New York, Continuum).

Inglis, F. (2000) A Malediction Upon Management, *Journal of Education Policy*, 15:4, pp. 417–29.

Love, K. (2008) Higher Education, Pedagogy and the 'Customerisation' of Teaching and Learning, *Journal of Philosophy of Education*, 42.1, pp. 15–34.

Ozga, J. (2000) New Labour, New Teachers, in: J. Clarke, S. Gewirtz & E. McLaughlin (eds), *New Managerialism New Welfare?* (London, Sage), pp. 222–235.

Preston, D. (2001) Managerialism and the Post-Enlightenment Crisis of the British University, *Educational Philosophy and Theory*, 33:3–4, pp. 467–82.

Santner, E. L. (2005) Miracles Happen, in: S. Žižek, E. L. Santner & K. Reinhard (eds), *The Neighbor: Three inquiries in political theology* (Chicago & London, University of Chicago Press), pp. 467–82.

Standish, P. (2005) Towards an Economy of Higher Education, *Critical Quarterly*, 47:1–2, pp. 53–71.

Torres, C. (1998) *Democracy, Education and Multiculturalism: Dilemmas of citizenship in a global world* (Lanham, MD, Rowman & Littlefield).

White, J. (2005) Education, the Market and the Nature of Personal Well-Being, in: W. Carr (ed.), *The RoutledgeFalmer Reader in Philosophy of Education* (Oxford & New York, Routledge), pp. 97–107.

Woodin, T. (2008) Managerialism, in: G. McCullock & D. Crook (eds), *The Routledge International Encyclopedia of Education* (London & New York, Routledge), pp. 368–370.

7

Militants of Truth, Communities of Equality: Badiou and the ignorant schoolmaster

CHARLES ANDREW BARBOUR

1. Out of Order

Any effort to come to terms with what Badiou's work on the 'event' represents for contemporary social and political theory—including educational philosophy—should begin with some consideration of the extent to which that work is *itself* an event of sorts, or has the features of an event as Badiou describes them. From out of nowhere, it would seem, Badiou and his growing number of followers have, in recent years, issued a challenge to a set of propositions concerning the operation of power, the status of knowledge, and the possibility of action that were for some time considered nearly unquestionable, and that in many ways defined what Badiou would call 'the state of the situation'. Against the notion that power is the inescapable condition of all social relations, or that society consists of struggles between a plurality of interested subject-positions, Badiou insists on the appearance of events that rupture with the routine operation of power, and militant subjects who combat power while remaining singularly disinterested. Against the assumption that all truth-claims are in fact thinly disguised power-claims, or ideologies reducible to the material interests of a dominant class, Badiou asserts the authority of 'universal truths', or absolute principles that exceed the circulation of opinions within a given situation. And against the supposition that all effective action involves taking a position amidst a network of power-relations, or constructing a convincing discourse that is capable of instituting hegemony within a limited political order, Badiou calls for the prescription of axiomatic statements, and the declaration of radical convictions that break with all established knowledge. In a manner that is often polemical, Badiou attacks the longstanding 'pluralism' and 'relativism' of contemporary theory, and its guiding assumption that both ethics and politics must take root in a relation to 'the other', especially the culturally or linguistically defined 'other'. More importantly, perhaps, he discards the familiar argument that a subject is constituted through its relations with others, or within a symbolically organized horizon, in order to privilege the militant subject who rejects all 'communitarian particularisms' in the name of her or his fidelity to a truth or an event, and to the arrival of its entirely unpredictable consequences. Refusing any curriculum, and any political project or ethical imperative, designed to achieve a predictable goal, whether it is the production of formally equal citizens or the inclusion of recognized cultural differences, Badiou maintains that ' "education" ... has never meant anything but this: to arrange the forms of knowledge in such a way that some truth may come to pierce a hole in them' (2005b, p. 9). Everything for Badiou hinges on the possibility that some subject will encounter some truth or experience some event and, on the basis of that encounter or experience, be utterly compelled to 'decide a *new* way of being' and '*invent* a new way of ... acting in [a] situation' (2001, pp. 41–42).

In one sense, Badiou's reinvigoration of the category of 'truth', after such a long and tortured hiatus, might appear at first glance to involve an extraordinarily rigid commitment to philosophy, and even a return to the comprehensive philosophical system. For Badiou, the separation of truth and power is absolute, in that 'there is no common denominator, and no common chronology, between power, on the one hand, and truths, on the other' (2006, p. 6). Insofar as it must operate in the world, or in a set of material circumstances organized by interests and opinions, a 'philosophical situation' always involves 'an encounter between essentially foreign terms' or 'a relation between two terms without any relation'. Between truth and power, an event and the situation in which it appears, there is no possibility of compromise, only a 'confrontation' that 'cannot be dealt with by means of arguments submitted to a common norm' (2006, pp. 3–4). Indeed, from Badiou's perspective, philosophy remains almost stubbornly indifferent to the machinations of power, to the point where the latter often reacts to the former with brute violence—the death of Socrates being, perhaps, the primal scene in this perennial struggle between the philosopher and the politician. At the same time, Badiou is not by any means a partisan of philosophy, or a champion of the contemplative life detached completely from the realm of human affairs. For Badiou, philosophy is always something that follows the eruption of a truth-event within a given situation. It has the modest task of, in a highly contingent fashion, nominating or formalizing the significance of a truth-event, or tracing out the finite parameters of its infinite appeal. 'Philosophy does not produce any effective truth', Badiou writes. 'It seizes them, shows them, announces that they exist' (2005b, p. 14). Truth, then, is not the result of a laborious process of self-reflection, much less something that can be arrived at through the protocols of instruction or submission to a master. Instead, a truth-event is something that almost miraculously happens, and that emerges in one of four aspects of human experience, each of which Badiou opposes to a corrupt notion that blocks the possibility of truth: love as distinct from sexuality; art as distinct from culture; science as distinct from technology; and politics as distinct from security, or the management of opinions. Thus we might say that, despite the highly structured nature of his arguments and claims, it is not a philosophical system that Badiou wants to construct, but a general anthropology of truth, or a hypothesis concerning the human spaces in which genuinely new events might happen and genuinely new truths might appear. In this context of this chapter, the question is to what extent education can become such a space of truth, or a milieu in which the experiences of love, science, art, or politics might find a place.

Given what has already been said, it seems clear that Badiou would object to two rather familiar educational philosophies, and treat them as means of preventing rather than fostering the arrival of truth. In the first case, Badiou is suspicious of any politics organized around the principles of inclusion or representation. Not only do such agendas rely on an understanding of politics as the negotiation of interests within the framework of an agreed upon norm, and are thus not political at all. But by suggesting that all subject-positions are reducible to interests, or can be located within a grid of recognizable power-relations, they also have the potential to foreclose the encounter between a disinterested subject and a spontaneous event on which all real political sequences are founded. For Badiou, 'the absolute singularity of an event' and the 'act of truth' that draws out its consequences, 'never' involves 'the plurality of opinions regulated by a common norm', but requires instead 'the plurality of instances of politics ... which have *no* common norm, since the subjects they induce are different' (2005d, p. 23). The logic of inclusion cannot account for the arrival of differences that rupture the state of the situation, just as the logic of representation, or the negotiation of interests, cannot comprehend the disinterested character of the subject who declares a truth. Similarly, and in the second case, Badiou's work constitutes a serious challenge to those who wish to ground ethics in an experience of trauma, or in the historical violence that has been imposed on others, and who construct pedagogical projects designed to sustain or recover the memory of such trauma. According to Badiou, ethics has nothing to do with being exposed to, or troubled by, the infinite alterity of the other. It has even less to do with a historical experience of, or a human capacity for, radical evil. Against what he calls 'our contemporary ethical ideology', which is 'rooted in the consensual self-evidence of Evil' (2001, p. 58), Badiou maintains that every ethics worthy of the name takes shape through a subject's fidelity to a good, and to a 'truth' that 'punches a "hole" in knowledges' (2001, p. 70) in such a way as to demand the affirmative creation of new ways of acting and being. Ethics involves, not vigilance in the face of the ever-present possibility of evil, or an acknowledgment of the precariousness of life and the mortality that haunts us all, but what Badiou calls 'the rights of the Immortal', and the assumption that 'every human being is *capable* of being this immortal' (2001, p. 12). Ethics speaks to the individual who has been gripped by a truth-event. And it has only one imperative: ' "Keep going!" Continue to be this "some-one," a human animal among others, which nevertheless finds itself seized and displaced by the evental process of a truth' (2001, p. 91).

2. The Axiom of Equality

While his work is often polemical, in considering his significance for educational philosophy it is important, I think, to take our cue from Badiou's call for affirmative inventions, and to ask what aspects of his thought might generate positive and new approaches to pedagogy and curriculum, or to imagine what it might mean 'to arrange the forms of knowledge in such a way that some truth may come to pierce a hole in them' (2005b, p. 9). In this case I would like to draw attention to what, borrowing from Jacques Rancière, Badiou calls the 'axiom of equality'. According to this axiom, equality is not a goal to be achieved or a regulative ideal guiding action towards a forever-retreating horizon of expectation. It is not social, and not objective, but thoroughly political and subjective. 'Political equality is not what we want or plan', Badiou writes, but 'what we declare under fire of the event, here and now, as what is, and not what should be' (2005c, p. 54). Or, put differently, 'equality' is something that 'must be *postulated* not *willed*', and genuine political action involves 'not the desire for equality, but the consequence of its axiom' (2005d, p. 112). Here, Badiou maintains, 'it is important to note that "equality" does not refer to anything objective' and that it 'is not a question of an equality of status, of income, [or] of function'. In this sense, then, equality has nothing to do with an equal distribution of concrete wealth or status. It involves instead an equality of intelligences, or an equal ability to think—a universal power to be struck by a truth. Thus Badiou concludes that '[t]here is no political orientation linked to truth which does not possess an affirmation—an affirmation which has neither guarantee nor proof—of a universal capacity for political truth' (2005c, p. 54). That is to say, every politics that is linked to a truth presupposes a universal capacity to recognize this truth. At the same time, because it has no calculable measures or objective determinates, the equality of intelligences or the equal capacity for truth cannot be submitted to the test of proof, nor can it be pursued as part of an agenda. It can only be axiomatically, unconditionally, and subjectively declared. It exists, we might say, in the effects of its prescription. Badiou's claim here borders very closely on tautology, although it is no less effective for that reason: equality exists insofar as someone asserts that equality exists. More accurately, equality exists to the extent that some subject acts and speaks on the assumption that equality exists. In either case, equality can be neither planned nor accomplished. It can only be practiced, and through this practice verified. It can only be practiced if it is axiomatically assumed. And conversely, it can never be practiced if it is axiomatically denied.

This approach to the problem of equality is so unusual, so unconventional, that it requires some elaboration. Importantly, Badiou buttresses his conception of the 'axiom of equality' by way of ontological arguments that I can only briefly allude to here. When Badiou posits a '*disinterested* subjectivity', or a subject that operates 'beyond the limits of interest' and remains 'indifferent to interests' (2005c, p. 55), he is not by any means denying the existence of difference as such. Rather, and far more complexly, he is proposing that no position within a given situation is capable of transcending that situation such that it might be able to categorize the infinite difference that constitute it in any meaningful fashion. For Badiou infinite difference is the banal ontological condition of any situation, or any given set. If a set is made smaller, or larger, it still contains the same measure of difference, namely infinite difference. Therefore, a situation or a set is not radically challenged or changed by the invocation of difference. On the contrary, it can only be challenged by something that is unknown and yet within the situation itself, or from what Badiou calls 'the Void'. The sudden appearance of this 'something' that issues from 'the Void', and that exceeds the recognized differences that make up a situation, is what Badiou calls an 'event'. The equality of intelligences implies an equal capacity for any subject within a situation to be seized by an event that emanates from the Void (see: Badiou, 2005a). This point is explained relatively clearly in Badiou's criticisms of Emmanuel Levinas's ethics of alterity, or the notion that I encounter another as infinitely other, beyond my capacity to comprehend. According to Badiou, this notion of the infinitely other or infinite alterity thinly conceals a theological commitment. 'The Other, as he appears to me in the order of the finite', Badiou writes, glossing Levinas, 'must be an epiphany of a properly infinite distance to the other', or an 'Altogether-Other' that 'transcends mere finite experience' and is thus 'quite obviously the ethical name for God' (2001, pp. 21–22). In opposition to this line of thought, Badiou maintains '[t]here is no God. Which also means: the One is not'. Instead, '[t]he multiple "without one" ... is the law of being'. Thus '[i]nfinite alterity' is not a mystery of relations with inconceivable others, but 'quite simply *what there is*'. Being in general involves 'the infinite deployment of infinite differences', which means, Badiou insists, that '[t]here are as many differences, say, between a Chinese peasant and a Norwegian professional as between myself and anybody at all, including myself' (2001, p. 25). Consequently, Badiou concludes, 'since differences are what there is, and since every truth is a coming-to-be of that which is not yet, so differences then are precisely what truths depose, or render insignificant' (2001, p. 27). Different subjects are equal in their equal capacity to be seized by such a 'truth'.

Badiou's approach to the 'axiom of equality', along with his assertion of universal truths, is not, however, a simple denial of difference, much less a reinvestment in an equality or universality that is objectively verifiable or transcendentally guaranteed. For Badiou, what is equal and universal properly traverses differences rather than simply annulling, collapsing, or dialectically fusing them. For Badiou, universality and equality do not imply identity, but an external term that operates at a 'distance' with respect to every particular. Indeed, Badiou claims that it is 'particularity' that involves 'an instance of conformity', in that in order to obtain it must define that which unites the differences that constitute it, whereas the universal always involves 'the trajectory of a distance with regard to a particularity that exists' (2003, p. 118). In simple terms, universality and equality are not unities, but radically open processes of unifying—not instantiated beings, but procedural becomings. Badiou offers two privileged examples of this process: the French Resistance to Nazi occupation, and, far more elaborately, the universal thought of Saint Paul. Referring to a comment George Canguilhem made about the mathematician and Resistance martyr Jean Cavaillès, Badiou claims that '[n]o group, no class, no social configuration or mental objective was behind the Resistance', instead they were 'resistant *by logic*' (2005d, pp. 4–5). In this sense, their resistance was the articulation of a universal truth precisely to the extent it involved a disinterested and absolute rupture with all of the different opinions and interests in circulation at the time. As a disciple of the Christ-event, or Christ's death and resurrection, Saint Paul is also one who holds in a disinterested fashion to a truth that traverses all law and all custom, or the established wisdom and the established differences of the situation. For Paul, the Christ-event has no proof, nor is it the proof of anything. It is, instead, a 'pure beginning' (2003, p. 49). For the same reason, it 'is offered to all, or addressed to everyone, without a condition of belonging being able to limit this offer or address' (2003, p. 14). This is the sense in which Badiou would like to understand the Pauline doctrine of 'grace'. Grace is universal and offered equally to all, not because it somehow comprehends all differences making up a situation under a generic category, but in the sense that it constitutes an impossible excess, an inexplicable supplement, or, as Badiou puts it, a 'senseless superabundance' (2003, p. 81). Traversing all differences, and irreducible to any given difference, grace is a pure gift, without reserve, and without any expectation of return. For this reason, it cannot be accounted for within the order of objective differences, but relies entirely on 'an immediate subjective recognition of its singularity' (2003, p. 22). For Badiou, then, the 'axiom of equality' entails each subject's equal capacity to receive something like the gift of grace.

3. Ignorant Schoolmasters

If we needed to draw a straightforward conclusion from Badiou's affirmation of the 'axiom of equality', it would be that truth appears, not to those who observe events objectively from the outside or after the fact, be they sociologists or historians, but to those who are subjectively engaged in truth-processes, or seized by events. As Badiou puts it, here quoting a deceptively simple slogan from the work of Sylvan Lazarus, when caught up in political struggles, ' "people think" ' (2005d, p. 31). That is to say, a subject's direct involvement in a set of political circumstances and their capacity to prescribe or state truths are correlative phenomena. One has an ability to acknowledge universal truths precisely to the extent that one has been seized or gripped by a singular event—resulting in the enigma of what Badiou calls a 'universal singularity' (2003, p. 22). No doubt many will hear in this association of a capacity for truth with direct political engagement an echo of the revolutionary enthusiasm that characterized so much of the last century, and resulted, some would argue, in the colossal tragedies for which that century will certainly be remembered. And in fact, while his estimation of the 20th century is far from laudatory, Badiou is one of the few contemporary political thinkers willing to face such accusations with an unflinching defense of the revolutionary tradition, or revolutionary sequences, against what he calls their 'Thermidorean' termination. Recalling the language of the French Revolutionaries, Badiou readily privileges 'the principle of virtue' over 'the principle of interest' (2005d, p. 128), and 'the aleatory trajectory of a truth' over 'the calculable trajectory of an inclusion' (2005d, p. 133). He privileges, that is to say, the uncertain moment of decision amidst the unfolding of events over the negotiated calculation of interests that seeks to include all established opinions. This, perhaps, is the place where Badiou's thought links up most directly with the question of education, for the 'axiom of equality' as applied to the classroom would almost certainly entail a repudiation of the notion that knowledge is something that might be possessed by a master and, through a curriculum of measured explication, delivered to a student. Rather, truth would only appear through an open educational process without goal or agenda, or in the midst of an 'aleatory trajectory' that risked the possibility of error at every stage.

Badiou's description of political action, or political organization, might even be seen to apply almost directly to education: 'Organized in anticipation of surprises', Badiou writes, 'diagonal to representations, experimenting with lacunae, accounting for infinite singularities, politics is an active thought that is both subtle and dogged' (2005d, p. 77). Presumably a similar organizational process in classrooms, and in the development of curricula, would allow educators 'to arrange the forms of knowledge in such a way that some truth may come to pierce a hole in them' (2005b, p. 9).

While questions of priority here are hardly germane, it is significant that Badiou develops his understanding of the axiom of equality in conversation with Jacques Rancière, and that Rancière himself provides one of his most comprehensive studies of this axiom in *The Ignorant Schoolmaster*, a book that seeks to revive and reinvent the extremely heterodox educational philosophy of the revolutionary 19th century language teacher Joseph Jacotot. The immediate context of Rancière's book was the somersaulting educational policy of François Mitterand's government in France in the 1980s, which oscillated between a paternalistic socialist agenda of inclusive practices designed to mitigate social inequality and a technocratic republican program of universal education designed to elevate everyone to the status of a formally indistinguishable citizen—what Rancière calls 'the pedagogy of the reduction of inequalities' versus 'the pedagogy of republican excellence' (2003, p. 221). Uniting both policies was the assumption that education caters to a lack within the student, or a gap between their knowledge and that of the educators. Against these approaches, Rancière reasserted two of Jacotot's axioms: 1) that 'all men are of equal intelligence' (1991, p. 18); and 2) that 'everything is in everything' (1991, p. 26). The upshot of these axioms is that education has nothing to do with an asymmetry of knowledge, wherein a master possesses knowledge that a pupil lacks, and that through stages of explication a master can impart to a student, but takes place instead amidst a 'community of equals', in which anyone has the potential to teach anyone else literally anything at all. As farfetched as this notion might appear, Rancière links it directly to reason. 'Reason begins', Rancière writes, 'when discourses organized with the goal of being right cease' and 'where equality is recognized: not an equality decreed by law or force, not a passively received equality, but an equality in act', or an equality that is 'verified ... at each step by those marchers who, in their constant attention to themselves and in their endless revolving around the truth, find the right sentences to make themselves understood by others' (1991, p. 72). In fact, Rancière goes so far as to suggest that there would be no such thing as society without such an equality of intelligences. '*Equality* and *intelligence* are synonymous terms', Rancière asserts. 'This synonymy on which each man's intellectual capacity is based is also what makes society, in general, possible'. For Rancière, the simplest act of communication presupposes the axiom of equality, which means that *if* something like society exists, *then* is must be based on equality, and not inequality. 'It is true that we don't know that men are equal' or that we cannot objectively prove their equality. At the same time, Rancière claims, '[w]e are saying they *might* be' and that 'this *might* is the very thing that makes a society of humans possible' (1991, p. 73).

Rancière's assertion that reason and society are synonymous with the equality of intelligences forms part of a larger attack on sociology, especially Pierre Bourdieu. According to Rancière, sociology relies on an assumption of inequality, or an asymmetry between its own comprehension of objective social conditions and the merely subjective understanding of those living amidst these conditions. By presupposing such distinctions, Rancière holds, sociology effectively creates the inequality it feigns to mitigate. While he agrees with Rancière's assessment of sociology, Badiou nonetheless insists on what he calls a 'radical discord' (2005d, p. 118) between himself and Rancière. Put briefly, Badiou believes that Rancière's community of equals is politically diffuse, incapable of opposing itself to any specific institution or position. For Badiou, 'every political process ... manifests itself as an *organized* process' (2005d, p. 121). If Rancière has a 'tendency to pit phantom masses against an unnamed State', Badiou claims, 'the real situation demands that we pit a few rare militants against the "democratic" hegemony of the parliamentary State' (2005d, pp. 121–122). The question here is whether or not Badiou's elevation of the militant, or the one seized by a truth-event, to someone able to discern the 'real situation' effectively reintroduces on another level the asymmetry of intelligences that Rancière rejects. What is the manifest difference between those 'few rare militants' enraptured by the flames of a truth-event and the mere interests and opinions of those mired in the knowledge of a situation? If we assume the equality of intelligences, not as a potential that might be rendered actual when any particular individual encounters an event, but as an axiom on which all social relations, and the very possibility of sociality as such, is based, how can we set about separating those who have heard the good news from those who have not, or the converted militants of a universal truth from the confused and opinionated multitudes? Here Badiou's invocation of Saint Paul takes on a slightly different valence from the one discussed above. For insofar as the militant refuses to capitulate to the realm of opinion and interest, or get caught up in the game of inclusion, she or he must operate at what Badiou calls a 'distance' (2005d, p. 149) from the state. But, as an '*organized* process', such a 'distance' can only mean the formation of a kind of para-instituion or minor institution that operates alongside the state, proscribing universal truths that, because it must seek to negotiate a plurality of opinions, the state itself can never accommodate. Despite the fact that he privileges Paul's 'antinomial' declarations and not his design for an ecclesiastical institution, what could Badiou's autonomous, organized, and distant band of militants amount to if not what was once called a church? Indeed, is there such a thing as an organized 'antinomial' subject that does not generate another law, another order, and consequently another realm of opinion?

4. Political Aesthetics

Badiou's invocation of an '*organized* process' and 'a few rare militants' who are capable of addressing the 'real situation' in his criticism of Rancière seems to withdraw with one hand the very principles that it prescribes with the other. In one gesture, Badiou affirms the 'axiom of equality', or the notion that all people are of equal intelligence. But in a subsequent move, he suggests that this axiom applies, not to the community in general, but to the potential that each individual has to acknowledge an event or recognize a truth, and thus become a militant who, once possessed by a truth, might see through the situation, or evade the opinions and interests circulating within it. Badiou is sure to present the militant organization as neither a substantial identity nor a formal contract, neither a social bond nor a political order. Instead, he claims it is 'the least bound place of all', where the only discipline is a 'discipline in process' (2005d, p. 76). It is, to recall, '[o]rganized in anticipation of surprises, diagonal to representations, experimenting with lacunae, [and] accounting for singularities' in a manner that is 'subtle and dogged' (2005d, p. 77). But, for Badiou, such an assemblage of 'a few rare militants' must be organized nonetheless, and whatever equality exists is first of all the equality that links them to one another as soldiers in the service of truth, pitted against their common enemy of the opinions and interests comprehended by the state. Rancière's approach to the 'axiom of equality' is of a different order, in that it locates equality in a different realm—not among the militants of truth, but in any society whatsoever, or in the possibility of sociality as such. Here we can see why, when it comes to elucidating the 'axiom of equality', Rancière pays such close attention to the problem of education. For not only is it the case that, as it is classically understood, education relies on the presupposition of inequality, or an inequality of intelligences, it is also the case that, in fundamental ways, all philosophical schools and political programs have articulated themselves as educational endeavors. That is to say, according to Rancière, pedagogy has followed politics like a dark shadow, marking even the most egalitarian social projects with an assumption of intellectual inequality, or a hierarchy between philosophers and scientists on the one hand and those they hope to emancipate on the other. Whether it involves 'proclaiming the universalism of the citizen and the promotion of the children of the common people through science and instruction delivered to everyone in the same way' or 'advocating a school and a cultural politics that [gives] high priority to adapting to the needs and manners of the disadvantaged sectors' (2003, p. 221), it amounts to the same thing: pursuing an chimera of social, material, or cultural equality by assuming and institutionalizing intellectual inequality.

If he affirms equality as the condition rather than the goal of genuinely democratic political statements, Rancière does not seek to depoliticize social relations. Instead, he claims that democratic politics begins with the assertion of a 'wrong', and the eruption of a voice that of those who, in the dominant order, have no voice, which is how Rancière understands the concept of the *demos*. The set of moves that Rancière performs here is complex, and requires close attention. On the one hand, he is rejecting the republican conception of 'formal democracy', or the notion that democracy involves the creation of institutions through which the formal rights of citizens get articulated as real and concrete. At the same time, he is also rejecting the socialist claim that a 'real democracy' must reach beneath such formal appearances, which are but a smokescreen in the service of the powerful, so as the reveal the material interests that are truly at stake. Referencing Plato's 'common battle against the *demos* and appearance', Rancière proposes that 'appearance is not the illusion masking the reality of reality, but the supplement that divides it' and 'that democratic appearance is not identifiable with the legal forms of the legitimate State that would conceal class interests and conflicts' rather 'the "forms" of democracy are the forms of dispute' (2003, pp. 224–225). The 'forms of dispute' that characterize what Rancière calls 'democratic exceptionality' involve 'neither the consultation of the various parties of society regarding their respective interests, nor the common law that imposes itself equally on everyone' but a 'litigious, "fictitious" supplement' to every '"realist" account' of political order. Insofar as it is concerned with appearances and forms, Rancière constructs democracy as a specifically aesthetic approach to politics. Rancière defines aesthetics, not as a philosophy of art, but in terms of what he calls a 'distribution' or 'division of the sensible' (2003, p. 225). Democratic politics is aesthetic when, through it, some *demos*, some subject that has no place within the established order of what counts as sensible, establishes for itself a new form and a new appearance, or a new distribution of the sensible, which it is able to force onto the public scene. 'Politics is aesthetic', Rancière writes, 'in that it makes visible what had been excluded from a perceptual field, and in that it makes audible what used to be inaudible'. Thus politics involves a moment of 'dissensus', or an antagonism that is not containable within 'the opposition of interests and opinions' but involves instead 'the production, within a determined, sensible world, of a given that is heterogeneous to it' (2003, p. 226). What characterizes democratic politics is the creation of new forms of sensibility, or new understandings of what counts as sensible. Thus for Rancière a political revolution is always also an aesthetic revolution, or a revolution in how we might sensuously experience our realities.

The assertion, then, that Rancière provides no grounds for effective political opposition to the state appears somewhat empty. Indeed, to the extent that he insists upon pitting a group of committed militants against the state, one could just as well charge Badiou with continuing to play the classic political game of friends and enemies, and thus remaining mired in the realm of interests and opinions that he wants to elude. The very 'distance' from the state upon which Badiou insists would seem to place him in proximity to the traditional concept of the political. Put schematically, and in far too simple terms, if Badiou locates his intervention at the level of thought, and explicates the 'axiom of equality' by noting that 'people think', Rancière locates his at the level of intelligence, experience, and the body in the broadest possible sense, and understands equality as an equal capacity to generate a new distribution of the sensible. The 'well ordered society' that Rancière challenges is the one that 'would like the bodies which compose it to have the perceptions, sensations and thoughts which correspond to them'. However, he claims, 'this correspondence is perpetually disturbed' (2006, p. 9). Rancière characterizes such disturbances in terms of aesthetics because he sees the aesthetic revolutions of the 18th and 19th centuries as revolutions first of all in what it means to perceive and experience the world, not what it means to create or appreciate art. The aesthetic revolutions generate 'a specific sphere of experience which invalidates the ordinary hierarchies incorporated in everyday sensory experience' (2005, p. 15). They make it possible to understand experience as something 'autonomous', and not bound ultimately to a reality that underwrites it. This explains why Rancière privileges the aesthetic speculations of Kant, and his proposition that 'aesthetic experience implies a certain disconnection from the habitual conditions of sensible experience' or a certain possibility of 'a form without concept' (2006, p. 1). Rancière's approach involves showing that this capacity for aesthetic experience is shared equally, that it is not the preserve of persons of taste, and that it requires no 'aesthetic education of mankind' to manifest itself as political. It also involves refusing every effort to treat the realm of aesthetic experiences as either the purview of an educated elite or an illusion that represses the autochthonic culture of subaltern classes. To the extent that there is experience, to the extent that there is a distribution of the sensible, and to the extent that there might be alternative distributions of the sensible, there is aesthetic experience. The fact that there is equality, and that this proposition is axiomatic, affirms nothing other than the existence of different forms of experience and appearance. It means that the multiple forms and appearances cannot be arranged hierarchically, and alternative distributions of the sensible will always emerge to disrupt or divide the dominant orders of reality.

5. Democratic Education

For all their many differences, what effectively unites Badiou and Rancière is an attempt to think politics without recourse to the category of culture, or to any substantial or formal conception of multiple subjects articulating their interests within the framework of a protected normative order. They both reject an understanding of social relations that, while influential for a very long time, appears to have degenerated into a toothless ethical pluralism on the one hand and a rigid politics of identity on the other. If we find, with Badiou and Rancière in particular, a return to the category of truth, which was previously represented as a thinly veiled instrument of power, it is by no means a truth that is either objectively demonstrable or transcendentally guaranteed, either scientific or theological. It is, on the contrary, thoroughly subjective, and has to do with an encounter with an event in the case of Badiou or a distribution of the sensible in that of Rancière. At least part of the reason for this reaction against pluralist constructions of culture and identity can be traced to the troubling failures of the deliberative models of democracy that went along with such constructions, and the betrayals of the great hope that, especially following the collapse of Marxism, so many placed in the possibilities of political forms. To take one example, Jacques Derrida's call for a 'New International', or a new era of international law that recognizes the need for 'force' but is nonetheless informed by a promise of justice 'to-come', seems completely fantastic today, when force has revealed itself to be the only arbiter of international relations, capable of making a mockery of even the most rudimentary principles of law or justice. Similarly, the optimism that many expressed in reformulations the meaning of citizenship, whether cosmopolitan or state-bound, must at least waver with the emergence of a whole range of quasi-citizen categories, used to exploit a transnational force of migrant workers. It is as though a longstanding commitment to difference and alterity has revealed itself to be incapable of much more than watered-down liberal tolerance, or what Badiou calls 'conservatism with a good conscience' (2001, p. 14). At the same time, Badiou's revival of militancy, and especially its Pauline formulations, while occasionally exhilarating, has clear limitations of its own. Despite the fact that Badiou tries to avoid these pitfalls, his privileging of 'a few rare militants' might be seen to threaten the 'axiom of equality' on which his politics is ostensibly based. As Rancière's work shows time and again, a genuine commitment to the 'axiom of equality' would require that we cut the knot that has routinely bound politics to pedagogy, and insist upon the absolute equality of intelligences. Only a politics founded on such equality deserves the name democratic. And only an education without preordained educators deserves to be called political.

References

Badiou, A. (2001) *Ethics: An essay on the understanding of evil*, P. Hallward, trans. (London, Verso).

Badiou, A. (2003) *Saint Paul: The foundations of universalism*, R. Brassier, trans. (Stanford, CA, Stanford University Press).

Badiou, A. (2005a) *Being and Event*, O. Feltham, trans. (London, Continuum).

Badiou, A. (2005b) *Infinite Thought*, O. Feltham & J. Clemens, trans. (London, Continuum).

Badiou, A. (2005c) *Handbook of Inaesthetics*, A. Toscano, trans. (Stanford, CA, Stanford University Press).

Badiou, A. (2005d) *Metapolitics*, J. Barker, trans. (London, Verso).

Badiou, A. (2006) *Polemics*, S. Corcoran, trans. (London, Verso).

Rancière, J. (1991) *The Ignorant Schoolmaster: Five lessons in intellectual emancipation*, K. Ross, trans. (Stanford, CA, Stanford University Press).

Rancière, J. (2003) *The Philosopher and His Poor*, J. Drury, C. Ostert & A. Parker, trans. (Durham, NC, Duke University Press).

Rancière, J. (2005) From Politics to Aesthetics? *Paragraph*, 28:2, pp. 12–25.

Rancière, J. (2006) Thinking Between Disciplines: An aesthetics of knowledge, J. Roffe, trans., *Parrhesia*, 1, pp. 1–12.

Index